D0906127

Our Friend, Jacques Maritain

Our Friend, JACQUES MARITAIN,

A Personal Memoir by Julie Kernan

1975
DOUBLEDAY & COMPANY, INC.
GARDEN CITY, NEW YORK

RANDALL LIBRARY UNC-W

B
Maritain

Library of Congress Cataloging in Publication Data
Kernan, Julie, 1901–
    Our friend, Jacques Maritain.
    Includes bibliographical references.
    1. Maritain, Jacques, 1882–1973.   I.   Title.
B2430.M34K47   194 [B]
ISBN 0-385-09659-3
Library of Congress Catalog Card Number 74-3696

Copyright © 1975 by Julie Kernan
All Rights Reserved
Printed in the United States of America
First Edition

B
2430
. M 34
K 47

Foreword

The philosophical and deeply humanist and spiritual concerns
of Jacques Maritain are to be discovered in his over seventy
books and in those of Raïssa, his beloved companion and wife.
They are, moreover, ably discussed by scholars and specialists
in the fields of his interests. But as the associations and events
which are the background of his thinking and writings are less
well known, these pages are written to give a brief personal
account of a life in which an intransigent search for truth
and a thirst for social justice were combined with a rare gift
for human friendship.

Jacques Maritain had a genius for friendship, so exceptionally warm, so disarmed and so disarming that he almost made
those who knew him forget his great accomplishments. He
was one to whom they could always turn, assured of empathy
and encouragement. And if he inspired and so generously
helped those who crossed his path, he in turn was influenced
and aided by others; especially in his earlier life, some of
these influences were crucial. He and Raïssa—for they are
inseparable—never forgot the friends of their youth and kept
them in their memories so long as they themselves lived. Later
friendships, no less warmly bestowed and warmly recipro-
cated, played so great a role in Jacques Maritain's life that
mention of many of them—all would be impossible—has been
included in this account.

To the glimpses the Maritains give of themselves in their
own books, I have added details learned from them in conversations, in their letters, in recollections of my own association with them and of others who knew them well. For data

received since Jacques Maritain's death I am indebted especially to the Little Brothers of Jesus, Monsieur Stanislas Fumet, Miss Helen Iswolsky, Madame Alexandre Grunelius, Stanley Vishnewski of the *Catholic Worker*, Mrs. Cornelia Borjerhoff, Dr. John U. Nef, and Mrs. Pierre Brodin. To my brother Thomas Kernan I am grateful for other data and recently published books and clippings he sent from Paris. For my interpretation of facts given me I alone am responsible.

J.K.

Washington, July 1, 1974

Contents

List of Illustrations

(Following page 96)

Jacques Maritain
Raïssa Maritain
Ernest Psichari
Charles Péguy
Léon Bloy
Stanislas Fumet
Jacques Maritain at the Sorbonne, age 16
Jacques Maritain at Meudon, 1932
Vera Oumansoff in New York
Raïssa Maritain, 1944
Ambassador of France to the Vatican
Lecturing at Princeton
In the Jardin des Plantes, January 1973
Coffin of Jacques Maritain in chapel of the
    Little Brothers of Jesus at Toulouse

Our Friend, Jacques Maritain

A Day to Remember

On that day of catastrophe in early June 1940 when the news began to trickle through that the Germans had crushed the French armies to the north and were moving on toward Paris, Jacques and Raïssa Maritain had come to my apartment in New York. (I had known them since I lived and worked in Paris in the early 1930s and since then common interests and ties of friendship had brought us closer.) For days the news had been alarming, and that afternoon they wanted to listen to the radio, for they had none in the hotel where they were stopping. With them was Raïssa's sister and inseparable companion, Vera Oumansoff, and two of our mutual friends, Father Joseph Ducatillon and Father Marie-Alain Couturier, from the Paris headquarters of the Dominican Order.

My own concern was deep, for I had a brother working in Paris, yet indelibly printed on my memory is the image of the two little sisters sitting on the sofa weeping, and the agonized faces of the three men as blow by blow the details of their country's disaster were blared out. "But where is our army?" they kept repeating, and rose one by one to pace the floor. Jacques's head, with its shock of graying hair, was bent, his thin figure stooped. Hands behind his back, he continued to listen intently in spite of his obvious anguish.

The Maritains had left France in January of that year. Jacques had given a course, as had been for some time his annual custom, at the Institute of Medieval Studies in Toronto, Canada, followed by lectures at universities in the United States. It was providential that he had brought with him his wife and sister-in-law, for they were with him and in safety when disaster came. However, his aged mother, Madame Geneviève Favre-Maritain, remained in her Paris home, and—despite notable divergencies of opinion—Jacques was linked to her by the strongest of ties and deep devotion. He had expected to find her there on his return to France at the end of that same month of June, but already he had been advised to remain in America and await developments. Now, in addition to the shock of his country's tragedy, he feared for his mother's safety; she was intrepid and outspoken. His sister Jeanne and her daughter were also in France.

That night Jacques cabled a friend in the Ministry of Cultural Relations regarding the possibility of his immediate return to Paris. The following morning he appeared in my office early, since he had asked for his mail to be delivered there. The cabled reply had come, but as he read the message his face fell. Under no circumstances should he consider a return, it said briefly. Jacques told me that the sender was a friend who knew of his speeches and writings against fascism, Nazism, and racism during the "phony war" and earlier, also that Raïssa and Vera were of Jewish extraction. All of them would be in danger when the Germans entered Paris, as now appeared inevitable. Jacques sadly admitted that the advice he had received was in his own interest. "If I don't go back now," he said, "I shall never see my mother again." And, indeed, he was right, for Madame Favre-Maritain died during the years of the German Occupation.

At the time of the fall of France, Jacques faced one of the harshest trials of his life. He saw his beloved country, so endowed with natural beauty, with art, with intelligence, almost as a living person, now "wounded, crushed, and unspeakably humiliated." How could a country that had taught liberty to the world come to such a pass? He could see no leader on the horizon to guide her through this period of darkness; his only hope lay in the French people and their ability to discern what was human, true, and free. As for himself, he was at that time fifty-seven years old; many notable achievements lay behind him, for this gentle, soft-spoken man had always been a "mover and a shaker." He had spent long years in trying to bring to others the truth of a philosophy based on the highest traditions of Greek, Jewish, and Christian thought and to apply them to social, cultural, and political conditions in the world of today. Now, with a future so uncertain, he had to restructure his working plans and personal life in a foreign country—which, it is true, he had grown to like and admire—and away from the home of his intellectual inspiration to which he had always been able to return as to a blessed haven.

Jacques Maritain was to meet the difficult problems of the years of his enforced exile with extraordinary courage and capacity for work and to make a valuable contribution not only to France's eventual liberation but to intellectual life in the United States as well, and to the aid of many refugee friends and scholars who came to this country. I shall write of what I know of these things in due course, but it is at this dividing point in Jacques's life that I venture to begin a more chronological account of his career and of the influences that shaped him, starting with those forebears who left an imprint on his character.

I

Early Influences

Jacques Maritain was born in Paris on November 18, 1882. His mother, Geneviève Favre-Maritain, was the daughter of Jules Favre (1809–80), the half-forgotten statesman whose position might be described as Left of Center in the political spectrum of the France of his day. Strongly democratic and liberal in his views, he was one of the leaders of the provisional government of the short-lived Second Republic, a prominent member of the constitutional opposition against Napoleon III, later vice-president and minister of foreign affairs of the Third Republic.

To President Thiers and Jules Favre had fallen the task of negotiating with the Germans—with Bismarck personally—in 1871 at the end of the Franco-Prussian War. Although they saved the key fortress of Belfort and succeeded in mitigating somewhat the amount of the enormous indemnity to be paid, we are told that Adolphe Thiers wept on his way home. For his part, Jules Favre resigned on his return, in protest at the onerous terms imposed by the victor, the most grievous being the loss to France of Alsace-Lorraine. He was a member of the French Academy, an eloquent speaker and writer, and throughout his life remained a supporter of humanitarian causes and staunch defender of the underdog.

Jules Favre died two years before Jacques Maritain was born, but he had strongly molded the character of Geneviève, the child of his first marriage. Raïssa Maritain writes: "As I came better to know Jacques' mother, I could admire in her a religious loyalty to the passionate ideal which animated the republican opposition to the Empire, an indomitable spirit of liberty, a fervent hope for the spiritual uplift of mankind, a boldness in her defiance of the world's opinion and a granite firmness—all of which never changed with the passage of time. . . .[1]

In his later years, Jules Favre, whose religion had been the agnostic Freemasonry that pervaded the Third Republic, became a Protestant under the influence of his second wife. His daughter followed him in this, and had her son baptized in her religion. Highly liberal, it required slight adherence to dogma, and advanced an elevated standard of morality based on the workings of the individual conscience. Although raised in Protestantism, the young Maritain found little to anchor him to it, especially when in the course of his studies he was exposed to the scientism that ruled in the intellectual and scholastic circles around him.

Jacques's father, Paul Maritain, a non-practicing Catholic, had scant influence on his upbringing. A Burgundian from Mâcon, he was a member of the Paris bar from 1862 to 1889, and had been Jules Favre's secretary. Easygoing by nature, his interests outside his profession lay in literature, especially poetry, and did not spread to the philosophical and scientific subjects that absorbed his son. After the separation of their parents, the formation and education of the two children, Jacques and Jeanne, were left exclusively in the hands of Geneviève Favre-Maritain.

In childhood, although Jacques's health was poor, his mind was constantly inquiring and perpetually in motion. He was thoughtful, an omnivorous reader, and from the first met with great success in his studies. Although his mother was pleased to see the gifts of her father reappearing in the boy, she was shaken at times by his fever for knowledge. To get him outdoors, she persuaded Jacques to take up sketching and

[1] *We Have Been Friends Together* (New York: Longmans, Green & Company, 1942), p. 47. Also in Image Books (New York: Doubleday & Company, 1961), p. 48.

painting. Although he did not develop this talent, he early came to understand a good deal about the techniques, mental attitudes, and problems of the artist—an understanding that he put to good use in later years.

Jacques wished to be himself and showed a sturdy independence of character. He did not relish comparisons—even in physical appearance—with his illustrious grandfather, whenever these were made by family friends. He later said that this was not due to pride or rebelliousness, but that "I had an inkling of a sort of fatal element of violence and bitterness on the one hand, mixed with much greatness and generosity on the other, in my ancestral lines."[2] Even if he tried to moderate a lively temper and deprecated his achievements, he always insisted on his own identity.

In those years the home of the Maritains at 149 rue de Rennes was filled with the comings and goings of friends, with discussions of political events and issues, of happenings in the social and cultural worlds. Geneviève Maritain, warmhearted and hospitable, welcomed them all, and Jacques's vivacious and brilliant sister Jeanne, seven years older than he, attracted a number of fellow students and admirers. Jacques tells that when things got too much for him, he would go to the kitchen to talk to the cook and her husband, a laborer, who liked to expatiate on his socialist ideas.

In his own quiet way, Jacques made warm friends of his own who, equally with his home surroundings, shaped his early thinking. When he was fifteen, he met at the Lycée Henri IV a young man, one year younger than himself, who was to be for some years his inseparable companion. This was Ernest Psichari, the grandson of Ernest Renan, the historian and critic. Renan was, in fact, the leader of an anticlerical school of thought which "dismissed Christ as God" and emptied religious history of the supernatural. For his

2 *Carnet de Notes* (Paris: Desclée de Brouwer, 1965), p. 10.

ever-growing troop, scientific and technical progress and the attainment of man's happiness through material means replaced belief in established religion.

In his old age, Ernest Renan's prestige was great, his days passed in the orderly comfort of a home frequented by numerous writers, scientists, and politicians. Ernest Psichari grew up in his grandfather's home, and although he had been baptized in infancy in the Greek Orthodox Church, that had been the end of any religious influence in his life. As Jacques Maritain wrote later: "What Ernest Psichari found in his family surroundings was a spirit of moral inquiry that was extremely broad and lofty, but foreign to all metaphysical certainty, and a marked tendency to ignore the conflicts created by the opposition of intellectual principles. You did not fight Christianity, you were deeply persuaded that you had assimilated and outgrown it."[3]

Since childhood, Ernest Psichari had lived in an atmosphere of liberalism and elegance. He was handsome, vital, argumentative, and passionately interested in ideas. He was also spontaneous and gregarious, and each year he chose with care a special friend among his classmates. It was a source of amusement to his family that at the beginning of every school term he had presented to them a different boy in glowing terms as his best friend and "a magnificent fellow." In the case of young Maritain, this sense of discovery was mutual, and Jacques lost no time in taking Ernest to his home to meet his mother and his sister. The Renan and Maritain families became close friends. For the next three years, the two young men were thrown continually together, taking the same courses at the *lycée* and then at the Sorbonne.

At the end of this time, Ernest Psichari met with a disappointment that profoundly affected the course of his life. He had fallen in love with Jeanne Maritain; but Psichari was

[3] *Antimoderne* (Paris: Desclée de Brouwer, 1922), p. 230.

only eighteen; she was twenty-five, and told him that she was planning to marry someone else. After this rebuff, the emotional young man left his home and family—despairing and penniless—to live through a period of debauchery in sordid surroundings, occasionally trying to find work as a laborer. This existence, naturally, only added to his misery. After two attempts at suicide, frustrated by friends, he faced life more squarely and accused himself of dilettantism and lack of self-discipline. He then decided to submit himself to the most severe discipline that he recognized: he enlisted as a private in the army.

During this trying period Jacques proved his affection for Ernest Psichari again and again, trying to find him when he disappeared, and when he located him, pleading with him to return to his family and friends. After Ernest's enlistment and departure for service in North Africa, Jacques kept in touch by frequent notes and letters, sending his friend reading matter and keeping him informed of changes in his own life and thinking. For his part, Ernest confided to his "old brother" the almost mystical sense of liberation he experienced in the self-sacrifice and obedience imposed by life and service in the desert. Jacques was especially moved when Ernest wrote that he had found peace in the conviction that "the submission of a soldier is the symbol of a higher submission," that, in solitude and meditation, during lonely watches and long reconnoitering journeys over the immense expanses of Africa, he had found faith in God and Christianity.

While still in Africa, Psichari wrote the books that recount the stages of his spiritual pilgrimage: *L'Appel des Armes, Les Voix Qui Crient dans le Désert,* and *Le Voyage du Centurion.* We learn of this romantic figure in other books. Jacques Maritain devoted to him pages of his *Antimoderne,* and in her memoirs Raïssa details the moving story of his conversion to Roman Catholicism. Henri Massis, another friend, published an excellent biography. Years later, at the Maritain home at

Meudon, I met Henriette Psichari, Ernest's sister, who gave me her volume of reminiscences of her brother. But even before the First World War, the *Centurion* had made a great impact on Psichari's countrymen and especially on young officers of the French army. He had become the very symbol of gallantry and patriotism, and the faith Renan's grandson had come to accept so painfully attracted the interest and practice of many who had been indifferent to it.

But we must now go back to the days when the young students Maritain and Psichari shared their discoveries, studies, and enthusiasms. Among those they sought out for lively discussion and argument was Charles Péguy in his "shop" of the *Cahiers de la Quinzaine* on the rue de la Sorbonne. Péguy was editor of the *Cahiers*, pretty much of a one-man paper, but one that by the caliber of its contributors and the passion of the debates it generated was a favorite among young intellectuals.

This paper was Péguy's means of livelihood and even more: he saw it as a vocation and the chief means of spreading his convictions. His own writings, most of which first appeared in the *Cahiers*, show him not only as a writer of genius, but a vigorous non-conformist who denounced the disorders of the modern world, the corruption of politics, the greed for money, and, as one who had been an ardent champion of Dreyfus, anti-Semitism in any form that it appeared after that famous affair.

Péguy's poems and plays—the first of his day to be written in the picturesque language of the common people—reveal the soul of the peasant stock from which he came, his love for the soil, his religious sense, his deep patriotism. Neglected for some years after his death, his writings were inspiration for many Frenchmen in their resistance to the Germans during their country's occupation. Since then his place in French literature has come to be more and more recognized, and he has become a cult figure to modern French youth, especially to those of the Christian worker and agrarian movements.

Péguy's personal life was filled with difficulties. He was quixotic and headstrong, frequently at grips with financial and domestic crises due to his improvidence, a devoted husband and father yet at odds with his freethinking wife, who did not understand his views and plans for her and their children. He was a friend of the sociologist Georges Sorel and at that time placed his faith in socialism, a doctrine that had appealed to Jacques Maritain since an early age. Péguy had left the École Normale before graduating, and had only contempt for the "historicism" of the Sorbonne, where many of his young admirers were enrolled.

Jacques and Jeanne Maritain had been introduced to Péguy by Robert Debré, a fellow student, who later brought him to the Maritain home to meet their mother. The writer and editor became a frequent visitor, and Geneviève Favre-Maritain formed a strong attachment to him. Although she was much older than Péguy, he called her "my child," and found in her a loyalty that never wavered. So great was the admiration of her son and daughter for this friend that they soon enlisted themselves among his helpers. Jacques aided with the details of production of the *Cahiers*, reading proof and carrying copy to the printer at Suresnes. For two years, Jeanne worked in the narrow, cramped quarters on the rue de la Sorbonne as editor of a paper for children which would carry Péguy's ideas to a new generation—until a dishonest bookkeeper, military service for some of the contributors, and her own marriage plans brought the publication of *Jean-Pierre* to an end.

Great as was Jacques's absorption in his studies and his friends, the greatest single influence in his life, from the age of nineteen, was surely the Russian-born Jewish girl who was to become his wife. At that time he already held his first baccalaureate in philosophy and was studying for one in science. Following the same courses was Raïssa Oumansoff, a slight young woman of eighteen with broad forehead and dark brown hair and eyes, whose quiet manner gave little sign of her burning intensity. For over a year she had kept very much to herself and had little to do with her classmates, "concerned," she tells us, "only with the professors, who without my even asking them would certainly answer all my questions, give me an ordered view of the Universe, put all things in their real place, after which I, too, would know my place in the world, and whether or not I could accept an existence that I had not chosen and that already weighed upon me."[4]

Raïssa was born in 1883 in Rostov-on-Don, the child of Jewish parents, who later moved to Marioupol, a small seaport town of Russia. In 1893, they had emigrated to Paris, bringing with them their two little daughters, aged ten and seven, so that they might enjoy advantages not open to them in their own country. Raïssa, the elder, had shown precocious aptitudes for study, and both in Russia and France had been given opportunities unusual for the girl of a family in very modest circumstances. At fifteen she had finished the courses offered at an excellent girls' school and was ready to prepare for entrance to the University of Paris. Since, in theory, her age prevented her enrollment for another two years, she was provided with tutors to coach her for the examinations in literature and the history of philosophy. Of her own accord, she read widely, especially the French classics, studied the piano, and cultivated an interest in music that never deserted her. At the end of a year she presented herself for the Sorbonne examinations and passed them successfully; she was then dispensed from the usual age requirement. Thus she was only sixteen at the time she entered the university.

Raïssa loved France and often spoke of her happiness when, in 1898, she, her parents, and Vera had received their naturalization papers and had become citizens of "the most beautiful country in the world." She liked to dance, and with her family attended gatherings held in the Russian colony of Paris. This

---

[4] *We Have Been Friends Together*, Longmans ed., pp. 38–39; Image ed., p. 40.

was, of course, some twenty years before the tidal wave of exiles who came to France after the Bolshevik Revolution. The Russian émigrés at that period were mainly anti-tsarist liberals and students, many of them leaning toward atheism and Marxism. Raïssa's hospitable parents opened their home to their former compatriots, and there she took part in lively discussions on social and philosophical matters. But she could come to no conclusions. She had come to feel that perhaps a knowledge of the physical sciences would give her the orientation that she needed. It was in this hope that she had enrolled in the faculty of sciences at the Sorbonne.

The friendship that was to become the great human love of Jacques Maritain's life began in the halls of the huge four-sided building that was the seat of the faculties of letters and sciences of the University of Paris. Its endless courts and corridors have been the background for many budding romances, but few could surpass the devotion that quickly sprang up between two young people of very different personality, temperament, and background.

Raïssa has told of their first meeting as she was coming out of a plant physiology class, wrapped in her thoughts and inattentive to the noise and chatter around her. She was approached by a tall young man, slightly stooped, with blond hair and beard, and blue-gray eyes. Jacques Maritain, doubtless at Péguy's suggestion, was seeking the signatures of French intellectuals for a protest against the ill-treatment of Russian socialist students by the tsarist police at that time. It was natural that he should appeal to a Russian-born classmate for help in approaching prominent personages in Paris. This aid was promptly given, and Raïssa came out of her shell to go with him to call on prospective signers of a letter of protest that Jacques himself would deliver at the Russian Embassy.

Into her fellow student's sympathetic ear Raïssa poured the questions and doubts that tormented her. Although her parents had ceased to practice the Jewish faith, they believed in God. Yet how could she share this belief? If God existed, how could he permit so much injustice, evil, and suffering in the world? She had thought that her studies in science would give her some answers, yet she was being constantly disappointed. All the subjects she was taking—botany, physiology, embryology—did not help her to know nature in its essence and *cause*. Her science professors, excellent in explaining empirical facts, considered speculative values as "mysticism," a field into which there was no reason for them to venture. As for the teachers of philosophy in the faculty of letters, although they were devoted and able, the system they followed was a historical review of the different trends of thought with no attempt to reach conclusions as to their merit.

She soon learned that Jacques Maritain's disappointment and perplexities were similar to her own. Yet, against this somber background, the two young people found joy in a companionship that soon became more and more frequent. There were long walks to and from the Sorbonne. There were visits to friends. There was an initiation into the world of art—especially painting—in which Jacques was very knowledgeable and into which he was happy to introduce his newfound and receptive friend.

Raïssa was soon presented to Ernest Psichari, whose high spirits and outgoing nature delighted her. She was also led to Péguy's "shop" of the *Cahiers de la Quinzaine* and was impressed by the commanding presence and zestful talk of the short-bearded man with the piercing eyes behind thick spectacles—the first author of her acquaintance. At the home of Jacques's mother, she saw Péguy frequently and learned of his domestic and financial difficulties, his aspirations, his yearning for justice and inner liberty. She soon came to share Jacques's affection for the older and more experienced man, who became for them a real companion.

For a time Jacques and Raïssa found another good friend in the ranks of their science professors. This was the biologist Félix Le Dantec, who invited them to his home. He was an outspoken materialist and defended his philosophy with eloquence. He hoped that these promising students would work along lines that he proposed, to demonstrate that life springs from some specific chemical combination. They were not impressed by this theory, for it did not answer their real question as to the *reasons* for that existence. Nevertheless, Raïssa was intrigued by Le Dantec's atheism, toward which she herself had been tending for several years. He expounded his ideas so forcefully yet so calmly that her self-confidence was briefly restored. Unfortunately, Le Dantec became quite attracted to his young pupil. Raïssa, not knowing how to handle the situation, felt she must tell him that she was secretly engaged to Jacques Maritain, and put an end to the association. She later expressed regret for her clumsiness, for she had valued the friendship of this kind and generous man.

By this time, faced with the enigmas and "absurdity" of existence, Jacques and Raïssa had become more and more desperate. What was the result of all their searching, thinking, efforts to understand? The failure of their studies in science to answer their questions as to the objectivity of knowledge, the low esteem in which their teachers held the mysteries of metaphysics and imposed on the intelligence the law of materialism burst upon them anew. One day they met in the Jardin des Plantes, that extensive park on the Left Bank of the Seine containing an extraordinary collection of rare trees and plants and different species of animal life. It was a favorite haunt of theirs, but this day they were oblivious to natural wonders. Now at all costs they must find a solution to the problems that tormented them. After a long and painful discussion, they decided that they would put an end to their lives if within a year they could find no meaning for the word "truth," and for the presence of so much evil and injustice in the world.

It is perhaps difficult for us today to understand the extreme seriousness, the philosophical absorption of these young people at a romantic age. We must orient ourselves to a period of time, and to a country, where there was no television or radio, no cinema or telephone, where sports were practically unknown. Fin-de-siècle Europe was a hothouse, racked by pessimism, the age of Nietzsche. To highly sensitive young intellectuals such as Jacques and Raïssa, the problem of man's destiny and the contradictions of his existence were just as real as the issues of anti-racism and anti-militarism have been for the young today. In their case it revealed the depth of feeling and a concern for the suffering of others that, directed in safer and more fruitful channels, were to characterize them for life. Raïssa's memoirs contain this revealing passage: "Jacques for a long time had thought that it was worthwhile to fight for the poor, against the enslavement of the 'proletariat.' And his own natural generosity had given him strength. But now his despair was as great as my own."[5]

Shortly after this, however, the young pair were to find at least a temporary answer to their questions. Charles Péguy had ceased to put his hope in the establishment of a universal socialist republic, and was relentless in his search for an ideal to fill the void. One day he led his young friends across the street to a lecture by Henri Bergson at the Collège de France.

This was not so simple a matter as it might seem and persuasion was needed, for the Sorbonne did not look with favor on the neighboring institution. The intellectual barriers between the two schools were immense, and there were strong differences in their educational purposes and structures. The Collège de France was founded during the Renaissance to encourage humanistic studies and was not connected with any other institution of learning. Its lectures were open to the public without charge; it held no examinations and bestowed no degrees. With such requirements removed, the range of subjects taught was in contrast to the established Sorbonne curriculum, the spirit of inquiry interpreted far more liberally.

[5] *We Have Been Friends Together*, Longmans ed., p. 76; Image ed., p. 67.

At that time large audiences—intellectuals, students, artists, scientists, and merely curious—were flocking to the lectures of Henri Bergson, the magnetic thinker with a new orientation who, opening a wedge against materialism and scientism, was dispelling prejudice against speculative thought. His first great discovery was duration which is directed in terms of life and is neither divisible nor measurable. He saw the world as containing two opposing tendencies—the life force (*élan vital*) which pervades all becoming, and the resistance of the material world against that force. To everything that imprisoned man in some determinism, Bergson opposed human free will. Man, he taught further, knows matter through his intellect, but is capable of perceiving reality through *intuition*. "The absolute," he said, "is included in the domain of the knowable—through intuition."

His eager young listeners interpreted this as meaning that through intuition they could really know *that which is*. It was not until later that Jacques Maritain began his criticism of Bergson's idea of intuition, mainly because the famous lecturer opposed intuition to the intelligence which forms concepts, thereby denying to that intellect the power to grasp spiritual reality.

However, it was in Bergson's smaller classes that they first studied Plotinus, the third-century neo-Platonist philosopher who spoke of the soul and of God. This aroused their interest in mysticism and led them to the door of a world they would explore on their own as they delved into Plato and Pascal. But for the time being they did not question the theories Bergson expounded with such eloquence. They exulted in the promises held before them, for they saw philosophy restored to its proper place and the possibility of work in the metaphysical field. In their hearts they already knew that this was work they would not pursue apart, that together they would share the search for that intellectual certainty for which they were hungering.

II

Love and Friendship – Pilgrims of the Absolute

Jacques and Raïssa's engagement to marry came about very naturally and early in their friendship. Because of their youth and uncertainties as to the future, they had not made their engagement known, intending to wait until Jacques had the *agrégation* in philosophy that would entitle him to a teaching post in a State university. Throughout two years of companionship and pursuit of mutual interests, this decision had remained unchanged even if, in a moment of despair, they had questioned their desire to go on living. But in 1904, they determined to marry without waiting for the end of Jacques's studies.

That summer Raïssa's parents took her and her sister to a small village where the family could enjoy the air of the nearby forest. Jacques Maritain soon arrived to join them at the small inn where they were staying. All went well on this vacation until Raïssa developed a throat abscess that assumed alarming proportions. Her sister Vera rushed into Paris for a surgeon when after some days the local medico had provided no relief. A painful emergency operation was performed and Raïssa was taken back to the city for a long convalescence. Although she recovered from this illness, her health was permanently affected and she was subject to many sicknesses throughout her life. However, by the following fall she was well enough to resume normal activities and to enter into plans for a simple wedding. She and Jacques were married on November 26, 1904.

Years ago, Raïssa gave me two pictures that have hung on the wall of my room ever since. They show Jacques and herself at the time of their marriage. Jacques has the pensive look of a young poet, his hand beneath his chin, a rebel lock of hair falling over his brow. Raïssa's broad forehead is uncluttered, her dark hair neatly arranged, and her large brown eyes gaze out with a look of gentle confidence.

This was indeed a marriage of true minds. Happier than they had ever been in their personal lives, the young couple found a small apartment near the Jardin des Plantes while Jacques finished his courses at the university. He obtained his *agrégation* in philosophy in 1905, and registered in advanced courses in biology—of all sciences the one that interested him the most. With household duties and precarious health, Raïssa was not able to continue her classes at the Sorbonne, but made up for this by many hours of reading; and when possible, she attended Bergson's lectures.

One day in 1905, impressed by an article in the literary column of a daily paper, they bought a copy of *La Femme Pauvre* by Léon Bloy, a writer unknown to them. This novel moved them deeply, not only by its tragic story of a woman of the streets, but because it carried a message of supernatural hope unusual in the literature of that day. Through it shone the writer's ardent faith in Christianity—a subject which Jacques and Raïssa had placed "in some realm of art and imagination." Wanting to know more of this writer, they read one volume of his published journals, *Quatre Ans de Captivité*. In this strange diary, Bloy wrote of the imminent doom of a world on the brink of disaster, of the sense of his own prophetic mission, of his impatience with the mediocrity of so-called Christians, and of his personal misery and isolation. In these pages he also divulged that his books brought in very little money; he was married and had two children, two others had died; he urgently needed help.

Moved by the sad revelation of Bloy's personal situation,

the Maritains sent the writer a money order for a modest amount, telling him of their admiration for his work, but adding that they did not share his beliefs. This literary beggar was not ungrateful and responded to the generosity of his unknown friends—who had very little themselves—with an appreciative letter and by sending them two earlier volumes of his journals. Soon they received an invitation to visit him. This they accepted with some trepidation, for Jacques and Raïssa did not know what to expect in one who, like Jonah, thundered so loudly against the contradictions and prevarications of the world around him.

However, on arriving in the humble home on Montmartre, they were immediately put at ease by an impressive man past middle years with white hair, a low voice, and deep-set dark eyes with their mingled look of melancholy and kindness. They found him in the poverty he had described, yet an air of peace pervaded the sparsely furnished home where Bloy lived with his wife and two little daughters. From the first, the whole Bloy family took the Maritains to their hearts. Of this visit Jacques wrote: "Once the threshold of this house was crossed, all values were dislocated, as though by an invisible switch. One knew, or one guessed, that only one sorrow existed there—not to be a saint. And all the rest receded into the twilight."[1]

The affection and interest with which they were surrounded that day were never withdrawn. With Raïssa's sister, Vera Oumansoff, they were soon included in a circle along with others who had been won by the sincerity they found in a man for whom God and faith, religion, and suffering were not abstractions. The harsh and vituperative language Bloy used in his books did not hide from them the grandeur of his intentions, his courage and generosity, his solicitude for the spiritual welfare of his friends.

[1] *Quelques Pages sur Léon Bloy* (Paris: *Cahiers de la Quinzaine*, 1927), p. 26.

Reading Bloy's works today, we are somewhat puzzled by their attraction for some very talented people. His polemical works contain many hasty judgments of men and events, his invective is often shocking. The novels deal with extremes of conduct and character, no place for the gray mortals in between. Some critics called him a "pamphleteer" and a "brawler"; they saw for him no place in literature. This did not trouble Bloy, for in a letter he wrote: "Art is not my aim, but is merely a tool that I have learned to handle and that I use like a sword or a cannon; I am above all and more than anything else a religious soul. I would give you all the artists in the whole world and all the masterpieces of art for the Lord's Prayer recited by a beggar standing beside a ditch."

At the Bloy home the Maritains first met the artist Georges Rouault, who, departing from the academic style of his gifted teacher Gustave Moreau, was trying to express his interior promptings in the choice of rare materials and techniques. It was one of the anomalies of human nature that Bloy—who totally lacked any taste for contemporary art—was horrified by his friend's somber and direful paintings of prostitutes, clowns, judges, shrews, and a suffering Christ. He did not realize that Rouault was following a path that he himself had indicated. The artist—withdrawn and slow to express his ideas in words—had difficulty in defending himself, but continued unhappily to haunt the company of a man he greatly admired. Their debates were followed with attention by the Maritains, always intensely interested in the founts of creative activity. As they came to know Rouault better, their appreciation of his work grew, and they were among the earliest defenders and exponents of the ideas of this artistic giant.

Pierre Termier, a distinguished geologist, Chief Engineer of French Mines, and member of the French Institute, often came with his family to visit Jeanne and Léon Bloy. It intrigued the Maritains that this courtly man was a devout believer and found no conflict between his work and his faith. Besides important scientific treatises, he had written books for the general public in which he celebrated the beauties of the earth, about which he knew so much, in terms that showed him to be a poet and a humanist. Drawn by Bloy's writings, he had sought their author out, and had become for him a staunch friend, often coming to his aid in a material way and encouraging him in his moments of depression.

Bloy's obvious affection for the Maritains drew Termier's attention to the intelligent young couple and he soon became attached to them himself. He took them under his wing, advised them on their studies, and invited them to his home. He followed their spiritual search with almost as much interest as Bloy, as letters that passed between the two attest. He was to remain their faithful friend for life.

Other friendships were formed at this time, but often in the earlier days of their relationship with Léon Bloy, the Maritains came alone with Vera to discuss their personal problems. Shortly after meeting him, they had read his *Le Salut par les Juifs* (*Salvation Is from the Jews*), and it had touched in Raïssa a particularly responsive chord. At that time neither she nor Jacques believed in or practiced the Jewish or Christian faiths, yet they were struck by Bloy's ideas concerning the historic mission of the chosen race. Had he not written: "The history of the Jews dams the history of the human race as a dike dams a river, in order to raise its level"? The continuity he pointed out between the Old and New Testaments, their union in the person of Christ, were no less a revelation to them. In an effort better to understand Bloy's allusions and symbolism, they read the Sacred Scriptures, with especial attention to the Epistles of Saint Paul. Not that they accepted the truth of all this, but they wanted to understand the motives and inspiration of a man in whom they found such great qualities.

Jacques and Raïssa were distressed that *La Salut par les*

Juifs, first published in 1892, had been allowed to go out of print. They had been so moved by the book that, despite their limited means, they decided to republish it at their own expense. In helping Péguy with his *Cahiers*, Jacques had learned a good deal about bookmaking, so now with great care he chose the type for a handsome volume to be printed in black and red. Léon Bloy was overcome by the tribute of his young friends. As he read the proofs of his cherished work, he insisted on dedicating it "to my little Jewess Raïssa (Rachel) whom her brother Jesus will well know how to reward."

Although they were much touched by Bloy's proofs of affection and the reading of his works, the road ahead was far from clear to Jacques and Raïssa at this point. They still could not share Bloy's belief in God or in the religion which he professed. Again and again they brought their perplexities to him. He did not attempt to argue, but patiently answered their questions. Little by little, he laid before them the fact of sanctity, and led them to books on the Christian saints and mystics. The beauties of religion began to unfold before their eyes and on their own they started to study the history, sources, and doctrine of the Catholic Church. By chance, they heard of the *Spiritual Catechism* of Father Surin, the seventeenth-century Jesuit; its reading drew together their "scattered notions" concerning mysticism and contemplation, and convinced them that one could not arrive at these unless one believed in God.

Now at last they "were brought face to face with the question of God in all its power and all its urgency," as Raïssa wrote. From now on the search had to be pursued apart and each in his own way, alone in silence and in meditation. Jacques, who considered himself to be an agnostic if not an atheist, notes in his diary that in November 1905 he began to pray in these terms: "My God, if you exist and if you are the truth, make me know it," after which he knelt down and said the Lord's Prayer. He later said that on that day he began to drift toward the center around which all else revolves. But even with the removal of his doubts of God's existence, there remained the problem of the true religion. He had distrusted Christianity because of Christians who had abandoned the poor and no longer honored poverty itself. How could he become part of a family of satisfied people who in quest of their eternal salvation did so little for the temporal welfare of men? Then, too, he felt that adherence to the indivisible whole of Catholic doctrine required a rational inquiry into its propositions and their acceptance. In becoming a Catholic would he have to give up the intellectual liberty he prized so highly?

Raïssa came earlier to believe in the presence of the Supernatural; a personal and what Jacques once called "a metaphysical experience" had convinced her of this. Yet she could not see why she could not accept the teachings of Catholicism without identifying herself with the members of a Church in whom she saw reactionary forces and much mediocrity. She realized, moreover, that her parents, who were Jews, would regard her conversion as a betrayal of their people and its sufferings.

The Maritains overcame these obstacles, but not without months of agonizing self-debate. In February of 1906, Raïssa was dangerously ill, and during days of anxiety Jacques's resistance gave way; he said that he was ready to accept Catholicism "if he must." During her illness, Raïssa had received great solace from prayer, and when her long convalescense began, she and Jacques had many conversations about the decision they felt they must make. They now thought that none of their objections to the Catholic Church should prevent them from following the voice of the consciences.

On April 6, 1906, they told Léon Bloy that they wished to be baptized in the Catholic Church. Vera, whose inner struggles had been voiceless, was present and said that she was ready also. Bloy's joy was immense, but not wanting to take advantage of their affection for him, he referred them to Father Durantel, a priest at the nearby Basilica of Sacré Coeur, for instruction.

During this period of study and waiting, Raïssa tells that they both suffered times of dryness and uncertainty. Although they recognized that they had no valid objections to the Church, for their speculative debate had ended, they flinched before what seemed a separation from the world they had known. They foresaw the disapproval of their families and friends of the steps they were contemplating. Even more, they feared that in becoming Catholics they would have to abandon forever their philosophical interests. Even so, they were ready to obey what seemed to them an imperious call, for they had come to believe that they would be exchanging philosophy for Truth.

Jacques and Raïssa Maritain and Vera Oumansoff were received into the Catholic Church on June 11, 1906, at the Church of Saint John the Evangelist on Montmartre. Jacques told that with baptism all their fears and doubts were swept away. Their godfather was Léon Bloy. It was exactly one year from the day he had the first letter from those he now regarded even more particularly as his spiritual children. Except for Pierre Termier, no one knew of the peace and joy they had found except their godfather and his family.

*

On August 25, Jacques and Raïssa left for Germany. After completing his course in biology at the Sorbonne, Jacques had been granted a fellowship by the Michionis Fund for a year of research in that country. He and Raïssa reached Heidelberg on August 27, and Jacques began to follow the courses at the university of the city. Of especial interest to him was the work of the biologist Hans Driesch, then formulating his theory of dynamic vitalism. Driesch's conclusion that life could not be explained mechanically or chemically was based on some years of research in Trieste and at the zoological station at Naples. Particularly impressive were the scientist's experiments with the embryos of sea urchins in which he was able to show that fragments cut at random always gave a complete embryo and the restoration of animal parts.

Driesch took a liking to the young Frenchman, lending him books and exchanging visits. Their discussions often turned on Bergson, whose *Creative Evolution* had recently been published. Jacques's hopes of a career in the philosophical field began to revive, although at one point he had determined to put these behind him. He tells of solitary afternoon walks in the snow as, after visiting Driesch, he sought a clue in the confusing labyrinth of science, concept, intuition. For the time, however, his absorbing interest was in his biological studies.

Raïssa's health continued poor, and in December, Vera Oumansoff came to live with them. From that time forward this devoted and selfless sister was a part of their household. She took care of Raïssa during her frequent illnesses; many domestic duties fell on her shoulders; she acted as secretary to Jacques and organizer of practical details. I remember that hers was the first voice—so like Raïssa's—one heard on the telephone; she made appointments, travel arrangements, superintended moves from one home to another. More important to the Maritains, her spiritual preoccupations were the same. Although not prone to discuss it, she led a full and devout inner life.

In Heidelberg the household of three lived to themselves, almost as a little religious community, following a schedule of daily church attendance, prayer, and spiritual reading. There were other mutual interests: first, news of their two families, who faithfully kept in touch. They were deeply moved when Jacques's sister Jeanne, whose marriage had been unhappy and who had separated from her husband, wrote that she had entered the Catholic Church, and that her little daughter Éveline had been baptized. There were books and messages of concern from Léon Bloy, admirable letters from Ernest Psichari in the desert, trenchant epistles from Charles Péguy. There was gaiety, too; Jacques was an excellent mimic, and the sisters found great amusement in small things, as when he read aloud to them in the accent of Marseilles. They skated on the Neckar, and there were walks along the winding river and an occasional visit to friends in the Black Forest.

In March of 1907, the routine on Gaisbergstrasse was interrupted by a disturbing letter from France. A friend wrote that Raïssa and Vera's parents had learned of their conversion to Catholicism and were in a state of great distress. Jacques felt that he should go immediately to Paris to explain, and was even more apprehensive concerning the reaction of his own mother, Madame Favre-Maritain. On his arrival he succeeded, not without difficulty, in making Raïssa's parents understand that they had not been separated in any way and in convincing them of the happiness that he and their daughters had found. Although they refused to discuss the subject of religion, he left assured that their affection remained the same.

With his mother he had no such success. To her the news was catastrophic: she saw conformity to a Church she regarded as authoritarian and reactionary, if not corrupt, as the end of her hopes that Jacques would follow in the steps of Jules Favre. On Léon Bloy she placed the blame of having literally mesmerized her son and his wife. Casting about for means to counteract this influence, she turned to Charles Péguy.

Péguy had always disliked Bloy intensely—both the man and his books—and had refused to meet him when Bloy made friendly overtures. In inviting Péguy to lunch with Jacques, Madame Favre-Maritain thought that he would add his arguments to hers. The meeting did not turn out as she expected. Although Péguy showed no sign of relenting in his antipathy to the author of *La Femme Pauvre* and *Le Salut par les Juifs* (he completely misunderstood the latter, considering the language Bloy had used in describing Jews as an insult rather than a defense of the members of the chosen race), he remained silent on the subject of Catholicism. Alone with Jacques, however, he divulged that he, too, had come to the same decision. "Christ's body is larger than we think," he added.

Jacques was overjoyed, understanding this to mean that Péguy was returning to the faith of his childhood and accepted both the doctrine and the discipline of the Church. This was the beginning of a misunderstanding that has caused the spilling of much ink and was being hashed over again in 1973, the hundredth anniversary of Péguy's birth. Judging from correspondence on both sides, and what is written elsewhere, what happened was briefly this:

Péguy's hesitation to take a decisive step at this time was due in part to his concept of himself as a leader of free men who placed their confidence in him. The subscribers to the *Cahiers* were his disciples; he felt that he must prepare them gradually for the evolution of his thinking, in the hope that they would follow him. His principal difficulty, however, was the refusal of his wife, the mother of his children, to accept his change of beliefs. A few months after his luncheon meeting with Jacques in Paris, he wrote asking him to go on his behalf to Quarr Abbey on the Isle of Wight to consult Dom Baillet, a Benedictine priest who had been Péguy's close friend since childhood and whose advice he needed now.

After some hesitation, Jacques undertook this mission and went to the English monastery where the monks of Solesmes were then living in exile. He returned with the message that Péguy should be married in the Church and have his children baptized. Madame Péguy refused, and since respect for the liberty of others was an absolute requirement for Péguy, he felt he could go no further. Jacques's attempts to intercede with Madame Péguy—inept, he himself admitted later—only worsened matters. The two men continued to meet and correspond for some time, but Péguy, offended at what he considered Jacques's doctrinaire position, in the end withdrew his confidence and they drifted slowly apart. Péguy's spiritual combat was to continue on for some years, until on lonely roads he was granted the great faith he had been seeking. Who has not heard of his pilgrimage on foot to Chartres? He and Jacques were fully reunited only shortly before the great war that was to come. Of this reunion Jacques's mother wrote: "Under the sun of that magnificent spring . . . the way of reconciliation opened; my son and he found each other in it. Through all differences, all silences, all separations, Péguy remained closely bound to his friend, bound by an invincible fidelity."[2]

*

The Maritains stayed in Heidelberg for the two scholastic years covered by the Michionis fellowship. The only break was the summer vacation of 1907, spent in Paris with Raïssa's parents. On this trip they made a detour to visit the shrine of Our Lady of La Salette in the French Alps and to join Pierre Termier in nearby Grenoble, where he had made arrangements for Jacques, Raïssa, and Vera to receive the sacrament of confirmation.

In Paris during that summer vacation, they had ample opportunity to learn of the reaction of certain of their friends to their conversion. Félix Le Dantec was quoted as saying that they had "committed intellectual suicide"; others said that they had "fallen into the hands of the Jesuits." They were accused of betraying "progress," of having succumbed to the "fanaticism" of Léon Bloy. Jacques's mother did not conceal

[2] Geneviève Favre, *Europe*, February–April 1938.

her disappointment, and although Raïssa's parents were as solicitous as always, it was obvious that they were not reconciled to their daughters' choice of religion. It is true that some other friends showed more understanding, but on the whole it was with a sense of relief that they returned to the quiet life of Heidelberg for the second year covered by Jacques's fellowship in Germany.

On their definitive return to Paris in May of 1908, the Maritains took a small apartment at 11 rue des Feuillantines in the heart of the Latin Quarter. Jacques was now faced with a practical decision of some magnitude. He had decided not to accept the post in the official educational system to which he was entitled by his Sorbonne degrees and subsequent studies. He did not see how, in the anti-clerical atmosphere of that time, he would be able to teach according to his convictions as a Christian. He was without resources and had to look for other means of support. Armed with an introduction from Charles Péguy, he obtained from the publishing firm of Hachette a commission to compile several reference books: an orthographic lexicon and a *Dictionary of Practical Life*. This was hackwork, but it left him freedom of mind to continue his scientific and philosophical studies and to work on articles that he hoped to have published.

Late that same year a new influence entered the lives of the Maritains in the person of Father Humbert Clérissac, a Dominican priest who became their spiritual adviser. A man of intellectual attainments and firmness of character, he was to be for some years their guide in matters of conscience and to play a role in their theological and philosophical formation. Raïssa, frequently ill, was able to take part only intermittently in the work of her husband, who, with Vera's aid, was spending long hours on the Hachette compilations. Unable to go about, she led a deep and secret inner life and spent much time in meditation and reading. It was at Father Clérissac's suggestion that she opened the *Summa Theologiae* of Saint Thomas Aquinas.

She had never been attracted by what she heard of the dry subtleties of scholasticism, yet she "fell in love," as Jacques said, with the *Summa*. Her admiration for the reasoning and exact and simple style of the writer grew as she read, and Saint Thomas became for her almost a living presence. She was no less interested in the life and poetry of the great medieval figure and regretted that his *fioretti* were not better known (this she tried to repair later in a book for children, *The Angel of the Schools*). She enthusiastically reported her discovery to Jacques, but engrossed in the work for Hachette and the writing of articles, he allowed a year to pass before he began a direct study of Aquinas.

This marked a milestone in Jacques Maritain's life. As he plunged into the task of familiarizing himself with the vast theological and philosophical system of the medieval thinker, he "discovered that he was already a Thomist without knowing it." In Aquinas he found a metaphysician of the intellect and reason who, following the methods and distinctions of Aristotle, adapted them to Christian revelation. Problems that had long puzzled Jacques were solved: nature and grace, faith and reason, science and the wisdom of the saints were combined in a synthesis that gave each its proper place, distinguishing but not separating them. He was confirmed in his belief that reason could be trusted, that it could be reconciled with religion and expanded toward experimental science, that the mind was lit by the five windows of the senses, and that the intellect had the right to feed on facts.

Jacques now had a yardstick by which all other philosophies—including that of Bergson—could be measured. Above all, he saw in the Thomistic doctrines a set of established principles for a new philosophical application to modern life. "Woe to me if I do not Thomisticize" became his motto.

III

The Young Philosopher

In his intensive study of Aristotelian and Thomistic teachings, Jacques Maritain had Father Clérissac as his mentor. Since the age of sixteen, this priest had been trained in the highly intellectualized traditions of the Dominican Order. "Christian life is based on intelligence," he often said. "Before everything else, God is truth. Go to him and love him under this aspect."

Although Father Clérissac's approach to Catholic beliefs was quite different from that of Léon Bloy—a Christian primitive who had little use for philosophers—the Maritains were devoted to both, seeing in them men of the Absolute who loved God and the Church and hated mediocrity. To be near Father Clérissac, they moved in October 1909 to 16 rue de l'Orangerie in Versailles, and for some months Jacques went each morning to serve the Dominican's mass and remained afterward to discuss with him theological and philosophical matters. From the first—and he never changed in this —Jacques wanted to be a philosopher, not a theologian, but he sought as complete an understanding as he could gain of Aquinas' teaching in both fields.

That year Jacques wrote an article on Hans Driesch's neo-vitalist theories (published in the *Revue de Philosophie*), and, at Driesch's request, the introduction to his *Philosophie des Organischen*. He then began to work on his first philosophical study, "Modern Science and Reason." He submitted this paper to Father Clérissac, who criticized severely the half-Kantian, half-Bergsonian vocabulary used, but approved it finally in recast form more in line with Thomistic definitions of "intelligence" and "reason."

This article first appeared in the *Revue de Philosophie*, and the editor requested two further articles on Bergson's thought (later included in Jacques's first book, *La Philosophie Bergsonienne*—1913). In spite of Father Clérissac's criticisms, or perhaps in part due to them, Jacques's talents as a writer and creative thinker had been quickly discovered. From the beginning, he showed many of the beauties of style which characterized Bergson himself in limpid eloquence and rhythmic flow of sentences. Yet Jacques's thought was his own and reflected his remarkably ordered mind and intent to examine every element of a problem.

The founder of the *Revue de Philosophie*, which gave the first hearing to the young philosopher, was Father Pellaube, an ardent propagator of Thomism, at that time receiving little attention in Catholic schools. Although as early as 1878 Pope Leo XIII had pronounced it to be the "official" philosophy of the Catholic Church, its study had been confined mainly to ecclesiastical circles. Most educators did not see how this synthesis of the wisdom of the Middle Ages, even though it incorporated all the science of the Greeks and of the Arabians, could be applied to the subjects covered in a modern curriculum.

Because of Maritain's enthusiasm for the philosophy of Aquinas, Father Pellaube recommended him for a teaching post at the Collège Stanislas, a prestigious boys' school with some fifteen hundred pupils. This enabled Jacques to give up his work for Hachette, which he was finding more and more irksome, and he happily embarked on this new undertaking.

Jacques often said that he had come to teaching through necessity, yet he was successful at it from the first. Even those directors of the school who regarded the enthusiasm of the neophyte of Saint Thomas as somewhat excessive were forced to admit that his students were not only unusually attentive, but passed their examinations for the baccalaureate with the highest marks.

Besides his courses at the Collège Stanislas, Jacques gave in 1913 a series of lectures at the Institut Catholique on "The Philosophy of Bergson and Christian Philosophy." They marked Maritain's first open break with Bergsonism and opposed the teachings of Aquinas to the thinking of a man he had long admired. It is often said that these lectures marked the emergence of what is known as "Neo-Thomism." Jacques did not like the description, saying that he preferred to be known as a Thomist pure and simple; he was not departing from Thomistic principles, only bringing them to bear on questions arising in the secular life and culture of our own day.

These lectures at the Institut Catholique were well attended and drew criticism as well as praise. In defending intelligence, reason, and natural truth, the language Maritain used was often fiery, a fact he deplored in later years and tried to correct in subsequent editions of his early books. Although he did not change his opinion of the loopholes he found in Bergson's system, he regretted his severity toward the great man, especially when after many years Bergson published his *Two Sources of Morality and Religion*, and told Raïssa that he and her husband had moved toward each other and had met "in the middle of the way."

Even if Jacques was considered by some as a "breaker of windowpanes"—a term he coined himself—he attracted many followers, especially among students. In contrast to the prevailing atmosphere at the Sorbonne five or six years before, a notable change in the attitude toward religion and morality was taking place in France. The young people in the *lycées*, colleges, and universities were now reading

Claudel, Péguy, Francis Jammes, Léon Bloy. Many had become practicing Catholics and there was an upsurge of patriotism. Among those who flocked to Maritain's lectures were numerous students of science.

During those years, the Maritain household continued under Father Clérissac's spiritual guidance, its members no less fervent in their devotional practices. Raïssa, still plagued by many illnesses, was turning more and more to a silent prayer and recollection, for little by little she was discovering her vocation to the contemplative life. This life both she and Jacques considered as the highest activity of those who were called to it. The dialogue of a soul with God is impossible to describe, but some insights into the thorny path she chose are contained in her *Journal*,[1] issued posthumously, and in those poems she permitted to be published while she lived. No age in Christian history has been without its travelers on this difficult way of contemplative prayer across "the dark nights of the soul," but it has usually been lived in a convent or isolated hermitage. What was exceptional in Raïssa's case was that she sought to follow it in ordinary surroundings and sharing the concerns and friendships of her philosopher husband. "It is an error," she wrote in her journal, "to isolate oneself from men. . . . if God does not call one to solitude, one must live with God in the multitude, make him known and make him loved."

Vera's spirituality was shown in the way of "a contemplative disguised as a sister of charity," as Jacques expressed it. Earlier, she had thought of entering a religious congregation and had also taken a year of training in the nursing profession at the Hôpital de la Pitié in Paris, but now she fully accepted her role in life as the care of her family and its ever-growing circle of friends. In 1911, her parents had moved to Versailles

[1] *Journal de Raïssa* (Paris: Desclée de Brouwer, 1964). English trans. *Raïssa's Journal* (Albany, N.Y.: Magi Books, 1974).

to be near their daughters and son-in-law. When, in 1912, M. Oumansoff died, his wife became a part of the Maritain household where, until her death twenty years later, this gentle woman was surrounded with care and affection.

Following his "mission" on Péguy's behalf to the Benedictine monastery on the Isle of Wight, Jacques had formed a deep attachment to several members of that Order, especially to Dom Delatte, the abbot of Solesmes, and to Dom Jean de Puniet, abbot of Saint Paul at Oosterhout, Holland. Drawn to the peaceful spirituality of the Benedictines—and with Father Clérissac's approval, which shows that the Dominican was not overpossessive—Jacques, Raïssa, and Vera journeyed in the autumn of 1912 to the abbey at Oosterhout. There they took vows as oblates of Saint Benedict, which meant that, although retaining their lay status, they would follow the rule of life and special devotions of that ancient monastic Order.

Later that year, Jacques and Raïssa made in the Cathedral of Versailles a vow of chastity in their marriage. During Raïssa's lifetime, this subject was never mentioned, but after her death Jacques wrote: "It was after taking long counsel with Father Clérissac, and with his approval and advice, that by mutual agreement, we decided to renounce a thing which in marriage fulfills not only a deep need of the human being—both of body and of spirit—but is lawful and good in itself, and at the same time we renounced the hope of being survived by sons and daughters. I do not say that such a decision was easy to take. It implied no scorn for nature, but in our course toward the Absolute and our desire to follow at any price at least one of the counsels of the perfect life—while at the same time remaining in the world—we wanted to clear the way completely for our search for contemplation and union with God; and for this precious pearl to sell other goods of great value in themselves. The hope of such a goal gave us wings. We also sensed, and this has been one of the great graces of our life, that the strength and depths of our mutual love would be infinitely increased by this."[2]

Silence regarding their grave decision was always maintained, but no one who ever saw Jacques and Raïssa together could doubt their great love for one another. Raïssa's admiration for Jacques, her belief in his genius, her constant efforts to be helpful to him in every way were obvious in all she said and did. That Raïssa was the light of Jacques's life was clear in his pride in her accomplishments and charming ways, his respect for her views, his concern for her comfort and health.

The Maritains' friends continued to find in their home the affectionate atmosphere, hospitality, and understanding they had always shown. To them Ernest Psichari came on his return from Africa to find the old companionship and to discuss the decision he had reached to become a Roman Catholic. Begging Jacques to introduce him to a priest who would understand his problems, he followed Jacques's advice and placed himself in the hands of Father Clérissac, who, Psichari writes, "encouraged me with an enlightened goodness that went straight to my heart." It was in the Maritains' little oratory in Versailles that he made his profession of faith.

Ernest Psichari led to the rue de l'Orangerie the brilliant young writer and editor Henri Massis, a boyhood friend who

---

[2] Note by J.M. in privately printed edition of *Journal de Raïssa*, p. 27. It was deleted from the edition of the same work published the following year. In his *Carnet de Notes* (Paris: Desclée de Brouwer, 1965), Jacques Maritain says that this was done on the advice of friends; that, instead of supplying a new note as they advised, he was including in his *Carnet* a chapter on "Love and Friendship" to explain the matter more fully, not as a philosopher or a theologian but "as an old man who had seen many things." In this chapter he distinguished the different forms of love, and makes clear that in no way did he consider intercourse in marriage as an obstacle to the mystical life or to contemplation. Yet he and Raïssa had come to consider that there was an absolute form of love—he calls it *amour fou* ("mad," or boundless love)—which one cannot hold at the same time for God and for a human being "even when, remaining within the bonds of marriage, they do not renounce that unique and sacred love of man and woman. . . ."

followed him into the Catholic Church. The Maritains took a great liking to Massis, recognizing his firmness of character and intellectual abilities. Massis was then politically free and independent, but often spoke of the ideas of Charles Maurras, the leader of the movement known as Action Française. At that time Jacques Maritain took little interest in politics, considering that his work lay exclusively in the speculative order; however, many Catholics who adhered to Action Française—despite Maurras' agnosticism and positivism—were among the Maritains' friends. Jacques was to become involved with them in a manner that he greatly regretted later.

The artist Georges Rouault brought to them problems of more personal interest. He had moved near the Maritains in Versailles with his wife, children, and elderly parents. They had met Rouault earlier in the company of Léon Bloy, but now for the first time came really to know this usually unsociable revolutionary in the arts, who came once a week to dine with them. Because they did not force his confidence, he talked to them freely, telling of his struggles for "an inner order" that would enable him to express in original forms his exasperation with bourgeois values and his intense religious feeling. To do this, he said, he had to depart from accepted forms of beauty, go his own way at no matter what cost, and accommodate himself to the consequent lack of understanding and to poverty. Through this friendship the Maritains were steeped in many problems of aesthetics which they sought to interpret in the light of Aquinas' philosophy.

Even closer in association at this time, more frequently in their company, were the Dutch writer Pierre Van der Meer de Walcheren, his Belgian wife Christine, a painter, and their little son Pieterke. Pierre and Christine were an unusually attractive couple, both tall and slender, fair in the Nordic way. Pierre's face was quiet and phlegmatic, although he had a lively sense of humor and frequently a lively twinkle in his blue eyes. Christine was red-haired, more emotional, affectionate in disposition. This friendship was for the Maritains another gift from Léon Bloy, who had led this second family into the Catholic Church in 1911 after Pierre and Christine had searched long and feverishly for belief.

The Van der Meers lived in Paris, but passed the summers near Bures, then a small village in the Seine-et-Oise, in a country house and garden overlooking a wide valley and the green hills beyond. There for several years the Maritains also spent their vacations, the two families living as one household. Christine and Vera shared the domestic tasks, while Raïssa spent much time with young Pieterke, fostering in him an interest in poetry, art, and music. A precocious child, he learned by heart the poems of Cocteau and Max Jacob; at Versailles he had played with the children of Rouault, and Georges Auric, often a visitor at Bures, gave him piano lessons. To Raïssa he early confided his intention to become a priest; she encouraged him in this, explaining to him the canonical hours of the Benedictines and other liturgical practices. The Van der Meers had two other children: Jean-François, who died in infancy, and Anne-Marie, born at Bures in 1912. Jacques and Raïssa were as devoted to these children as though they were their own.

The families living together at Bures were fervent in their religious devotions, still strongly under the influence of Léon Bloy. Everything that happened in the lives of his spiritual children was to their godfather an event that affected him personally. Even though, in May 1911, Bloy and his family had left Montmartre and moved to the suburb of Bourg-la-Reine, this did not prevent him from keeping in close touch with the Maritains and Van der Meers. When they could not come to Bourg-la-Reine, Bloy would journey to Bures or to Versailles. These visits with their godfather, wherever they took place, were always remembered by the members of the two families as a source of inspiration and delight.

*

With the outbreak of the First World War in 1914, the Maritains were not spared the losses and changes inflicted on their compatriots. Although aware of the diplomatic maneuvers and political turmoil of the preceding months, a full-scale European war was to them unthinkable. They learned of the outbreak of hostilities while at the Benedictine abbey on the Isle of Wight, where they had gone on a visit at the invitation of the monks and, in "indescribable anguish and stupor at what had happened," stayed on for some time to pray with the community.

Both Ernest Psichari and Charles Péguy were mobilized and left for the front on August 6, two days after the declaration of war. Péguy, who took very seriously his duties as a reserve officer, spent his last night in Paris at the home of Jacques's mother. Filled with confidence in the successful outcome of the conflict, he said to Madame Favre-Maritain as he left: "I leave as a soldier of the Republic, for general disarmament and the last of wars," somehow managing to instill a measure of hope in his faithful friend.

Alas, three weeks later Ernest Psichari was killed at Rossignol near the Belgian frontier. On September 5, Péguy met the same fate in the battle of the Marne as he led an attack on the Germans in the neighborhood of Villeroy. In November, another blow fell: Father Clérissac, the Maritains' beloved spiritual guide, died is Angers. Jacques and Raïssa thus lost three of their closest friends at the very beginning of the war.

Immediately on returning to France from the Isle of Wight, Jacques had presented himself to a draft board. Since, however, a medical examination revealed a weakness of the lungs, the result of a severe attack of pleurisy in childhood, he was placed on the suspended list. He therefore tried to make himself useful in civilian life. As the war had brought about a great shortage of teachers, he redoubled his work. He resumed his courses at the Institut Catholique and, in 1915–16, again taught at the Collège Stanislas and, in 1916–17, at the preparatory seminary in Versailles.

To these activities Jacques added the preparation of a manual of philosophy for the use of seminaries. This was undertaken at the request of Monseigneur Baudrillart and other trustees of the Institut Catholique, in support of a similar request from the Congregation of Seminaries and Universities in Rome. Jacques took much pains with this task, for he wanted a new presentation, one based on his teaching experience, and sufficiently condensed to cover the courses prescribed. As quickly as possible he produced the first version of his *Introduction to Philosophy* (to be revised many times later as it came into broader use), clearly written and newly arranged. In it, he brought forward at once a general outline of principal problems and suggested solutions in keeping with the Thomistic spirit and method. In May 1917, he was agreeably surprised to receive from Rome word that the Congregation of Seminaries and Universities had granted him an honorary doctorate of philosophy.

In August of that year, Jacques was pronounced "fit for military service" and assigned to the 81st Artillery Regiment at Versailles. He always referred to this episode with amusement, for he told that after a medical examination he was placed under observation for two weeks. He was provided with a ragged uniform, and directed to take no part in the training exercises until the medical report was received. So after reveille each morning, there was nothing for him to do but remain in the barracks; he therefore spent the time putting down notes for a book on Descartes. When the two weeks were up, he was deferred for another year—at which time the nerve-wracking performance was repeated.

As the long holocaust dragged on, there was increasing danger from bombings by the long-range Big Bertha guns and from the Gotha airplanes hovering over the Paris region. Versailles seemed no longer safe, and Jacques and Pierre Van der Meer kept their families at Bures, their summer retreat, ten miles from the city and accessible by a little train. The two men joined them as frequently as possible, going into Paris—Jacques to teach and Pierre to work as a war correspondent—but they often had to spend the night at Versailles. Pierre Van der Meer tells of a night in a cellar, during an air alarm, when he and Jacques passed the hours reading in turn to one another extracts from *La Femme Pauvre*. Familiar as they were, the language and ideas of Bloy held their attention during the hours of tension.

In the spring of 1918, even Bures was too close to Paris for comfort. Jacques moved Vera and her mother farther away, to Vernie, a small village in the *département* of the Sarthe, where they had been invited to stay with the local curé, Abbé Gouin, in his large, rambling rectory in the shadow of the church. Raïssa did not go with them, for she and Jacques were setting out in the midst of the war on a great adventure—their first visit to Rome.

Jacques had written a long work on the apparitions of the Virgin of Salette, to whom both he and Raïssa had great devotion. This manuscript he wished to submit to the Roman ecclesiastical authorities, who had the matter under study and who, he found, had reservations about the advisability of its publication at that time. The trip, however, had many compensations. Jacques and Raïssa were paternally received in private audience by Pope Benedict XV and Jacques was able to meet and discuss Thomistic questions with the leading specialists in Rome. Among these was a noted theologian, Father Garrigou-Lagrange, at the Dominican college of the Angelicum, who was to prove his friendship over many years thereafter.

On their return to France, Jacques took Raïssa to Vernie and then resumed his classwork in Paris in the midst of bombs and shells. Vernie was too far for him to commute, but after several months, at the end of the school year, he rejoined the household at Vernie. He was to remain there for some time, for he had been given a year's leave of absence by the Institut Catholique to work further on his *Introduction to Philosophy* and the preparation of his little book on logic. And although Raïssa was often ill at Vernie, she and Jacques worked together on the writing of one of his most influential books: *Art and Scholasticism.*

During this time Jacques had occasionally to return to Paris or Versailles on matters connected with his writings or personal affairs (among them his military service). Still he was able to spend most of the time with his family and to share the company of the amiable Abbé Gouin. There was other companionship, for the hospitable priest had also invited Pierre Van der Meer and his family to stay with him. Their lives together went on as at Bures until September of 1918, when the Van der Meers returned to Pierre's native Holland. The Maritains were to stay at Vernie after the signing of the armistice and did not go back to their home at Versailles until the beginning of the fall academic term of 1919. In the meantime much had happened.

During the war, Léon Bloy had continued to live at Bourg-la-Reine. Terribly depressed by the apocalypse he had long predicted, he was still in destitution and forced himself to go on writing book after book. Jacques and Raïssa spent several weeks with him in the summer of 1917, and saw with sorrow that his health was falling fast. He was very feeble, but insisted on going each morning to church with Jacques. "I can still see him in the gray light of early morning—at that hour when the heart, 'not yet sullied by the base enchantment of light, reaches out toward the quiet tabernacle'—

walking with his heavy tired step to the first mass," Jacques recalled in his *Quelques Pages sur Léon Bloy*.

In the fall of that year Bloy was struck down by a painful illness. During his last days, Raïssa was constantly at his bedside and has written movingly of that time in her memoirs. She tells of her impression that during this week of agony he was struggling *alone* "in the ante-room of God," never faltering in the unshakable strength of his religious fervor. On November 1, Bloy received communion for the last time; those present were his wife and daughters, Pierre Termier, Raïssa, Vera, and Jacques. Their great friend passed away on the evening of November 3, 1917. Jacques spent the night in prayer beside the body of one to whom, after God, he felt that he owed the greatest gift of his life: his faith.

Jacques and Raïssa venerated Bloy's memory as long as they lived. I can still see Raïssa in New York during the Second World War, working long hours as she selected passages from Bloy's prolific writings for a four-hundred-page translation into English. And Jacques was again working on reminiscences of Léon Bloy during the last year of his own life.

*

As if to console them for so many sad losses, the war years brought other precious friendships to the Maritains. Of these, two were outstanding. One brought spiritual and intellectual help; the second, a most unexpected material endowment.

Among those who attended Jacques's lectures at the Institut Catholique in November 1915 was Father Pierre Dehau, another son of Dominic and Aquinas, known for his theological and spiritual writings. Father Clérissac had been called to Angers, and although he kept in touch with his spiritual protégés until his death, it was a relief to have someone nearer at hand to discuss their problems. Father Dehau's guidance was especially welcome to Raïssa, for he understood better than Father Clérissac her desire to lead a life of "contempla-

tion on the roads" of the world. Vera was also more at ease
with him. As for Jacques, he found in Father Dehau's learning
and perception an invaluable aid in his Thomistic studies. For
twenty-five years, until he was incapacitated by ill health,
Father Dehau continued to advise him on difficult philosophical and theological problems. Somewhat disguised—because
he never wished to be mentioned—he was the Théonas of
the book on Thomistic questions which Jacques published
in 1921.

As for the second new friend referred to above: In the
midst of the war, Jacques received a moving letter from a
soldier recovering from a wound in a hospital at Nice. Jacques
did not know the writer, one Pierre Villard, but the letter
stated that two years earlier he had attended some of Jacques's
lectures. He was getting in touch with him now because, in
his "deep intellectual isolation," the war had brought about a
crisis in his hopes for a better temporal world for humanity,
and he was drifting in the worst moral uncertainty.

He turned to Jacques, he said, because he saw in him a
"philosopher following with a lucid eye the chain of cause
and effect," and a man who faced with courage the difficult
problems of life. In the intellectual order, Villard said, he
had in the past most admired the ideas of Charles Maurras,
Georges Sorel, and Pascal. From the first of this disparate
trio, he had derived his definition of order, the idea that
men are governed by tradition, and a sense of the historical
destiny of France. In the second, he had found congenial a
concern for the moral and cultural development of the human
spirit. Finally, to Pascal he owed the revelation of the soul,
"the only living principle capable of introducing a little order
into our chaos." Despite his attraction to these ideas, Villard
said that he could not find a way to coordinate them within
himself. Would Jacques receive him as he passed through
Paris on his way to rejoin his regiment?

Although well occupied with teaching and family cares,

Jacques at once answered the cry for help. In his diary for April 21, 1917, he notes: "Visit from Pierre Villard. In this poor soldier with the meditative face, one senses a soul thirsting for purity and the absolute, one who has come to the belief that the greatest need is to *feel* the things of the spirit, and whom the loss of faith (if he has really lost it) has left in a state of vacillation beyond remedy."[3]

Jacques saw Pierre Villard three or four times afterward, as the soldier passed through Paris on leave. In addition to this, they began a long and remarkable correspondence which revealed the high aspirations and moral preoccupations of Pierre Villard and Jacques's helpfulness to those—however humble and unknown—who turned to him in need. Twenty-three of Pierre Villard's letters—some written on the eve of battle—and copies of Jacques's replies and pertinent entries in his diary still exist in the Maritain Center of Studies at Kolbsheim, Alsace.

Pierre Villard was killed on June 28, 1918. In August of that year Jacques was stupefied to receive from a lawyer in Nancy a letter saying that, according to the terms of his will, Pierre Villard's fortune was to be divided equally between himself and Charles Maurras. The man Jacques had believed to be of very modest means was, in fact, the heir to a large estate which he wished to "contribute to the safeguard of what remains of the moral and intellectual patrimony of our country." Each of the heirs was to be left completely free as to the manner in which he would spend the bequest.

Jacques was overcome both by this generosity and by the responsibility it entailed. He had no desire to change his way of life. He and Raïssa had always lived on a very modest scale; they did not like any sign of luxury or ostentation. On the other hand, the salaries paid to the professors at the Institut Catholique—never an affluent institution—were

---

[3] *Carnet de Notes*, p. 147.

modest, to say the least; Jacques had little time or freedom of movement for the broader efforts to which he wanted to devote himself. There were the books he planned to write, the wider contacts in the cultural field, perhaps extending to countries other than France.

Finally, after long hesitation and consultation with those he trusted, he accepted Pierre Villard's legacy. He was in this way enabled to shorten his hours of teaching, and although he continued for some years to give courses at the Institut Catholique, he no longer accepted a salary. This was turned over to a promising young philosopher who replaced him in some of his classes. Jacques thought that the financial aid from Pierre Villard would enable him and Raïssa—whose health had always to be considered—to live in reasonable comfort until such time as he would earn a sufficient income from his writing and lecturing.

In considering how best to use the resources so unexpectedly placed in his hands, Jacques decided that he should apply them to further efforts in the philosophical and cultural order, and to establish some kind of center for the spread of the philosophical and spiritual influence of Saint Thomas. He therefore turned to an idea that he and Raïssa had long held in mind. It was to start a "Cercle Thomiste," or center for Thomistic study. Much as they cherished their privacy and the time for meditation, study, and writing, they felt that they must share with others a knowledge of Aquinas' teachings and open the doors of their home to all who came.

IV

The Thomist Centers – Meudon

The idea of meetings for philosophical study was not new with Jacques and Raïssa Maritain. Even before the First World War, they had held a study session of this kind in their new home in Versailles at 21 rue Baillet-Reviron, where they moved in 1913. Plans to continue had to be put aside, along with many others, during the anxieties and dislocations of the four years of hostilities.

On their return to Versailles in the fall of 1919, they began at once to hold monthly meetings—today we would call them seminars—for the study of Thomistic philosophy, attended at first by a few of their personal friends and some of Jacques's students at the Institut Catholique. These meetings were to grow in size with the passing of each month and year. When I went to them in the early 1930s, some forty to fifty persons came.

From the first, they were held on Sunday afternoons in the informal atmosphere of a home, and they never lost this quality. Everyone was made welcome on arrival, introduced to the others. Raïssa and Vera served tea. For the discussions, Jacques prepared an outline in advance, but did not give a formal lecture, merely reading and briefly explaining the texts under consideration and answering questions addressed to him. Each one present was encouraged to speak and was listened to attentively. Those who knew Jacques only as a positive philosopher and fiery lecturer were often surprised at his restrained, almost timid manner, but were invariably drawn to the man with the thoughtful face and kindly ways. Raïssa and Vera moved about, putting their guests at ease, Raïssa bringing up a point now and then to further the discussion. Most of the guests left before dinnertime, but a few always lingered on for the meal, talking until late in the evening.

As the Maritains gained experience from these meetings, they drew up bylaws for a more definite organization of the first Thomist Center and for similar ones that they hoped to see established elsewhere. The purpose of the Centers was stated to be the grouping of men of good will, especially laymen, who wished to work for the diffusion of the Thomistic doctrine at a time when there was great need for a general philosophical orientation. Preparation for this would involve not only familiarity with Thomistic principles, but their application to discoveries in different fields since Aquinas' day, and to the intellectual renaissance taking place in arts and letters.

As disciples of Saint Thomas who kept in mind the desirable unity between the work of the intellect and spiritual life, the Maritains proposed in their plan the study of the theology as well as the philosophy of Aquinas, also some definite commitment to prayer and meditation on the part of members of the Centers. Each Center had a director, but their over-all intellectual and spiritual guidance was placed in the hands of the Dominican Order. The first general director to be appointed was the theologian Father Garrigou-Lagrange (whom they had met at the Angelicum in Rome), and yearly reports were to be made to him. He was already a good friend of Jacques's and Raïssa's and deeply interested in their undertaking.

In addition to the monthly meetings of the Centers, the bylaws also provided for annual spiritual retreats for those members who wished to attend. For the retreats of the first Center—for there were soon others in England, Switzerland, and Belgium—the Maritain home served as headquarters, and Father Garrigou-Lagrange usually appeared to preach. Even for the first retreat, held at Versailles in 1922, far too many applied for the Maritains to take them under their roof; lodgings had to be found in neighboring religious institutions, while arrangements for the sermons and religious services were made in nearby parish halls and chapels. All this involved a vast amount of preparation (letter writing, invitations, provision of meals, allocation of rooms). In these preparations Raïssa and Vera played a major role, as Jacques was teaching, working on his books, and often away giving lectures.

As the house in Versailles became too small for these activities, it was necessary for the Maritains to look for more spacious quarters. In the spring of 1923, Raïssa was again too ill to take a part in the search, but Vera found at Meudon, a suburban town between Paris and Versailles, a property admirably suited to their needs; an unpretentious stone villa with a large number of rooms and a small garden, protected from the street by a stone wall, and behind it a parapet from which one could look down on Paris with Sacré Coeur and the Eiffel Tower in the distance. Jacques came next day to see this property, and made arrangements to purchase it with a portion of the legacy from Pierre Villard.

The house in Meudon was to be the Maritains' home for the next sixteen years, years Raïssa later described as "the sunny days of France." Even though at Meudon she was to know much suffering, both physical and spiritual, it was the only place, Jacques tells us, that "she felt herself a little sheltered on earth." She spent many hours in her little study with its glazed window opening into the chapel, where permission had been given for the Blessed Sacrament to be kept; from time to time she would go into the chapel to pray close to the altar. After the hours spent in this way she would emerge to deal gently and quietly with whatever task was at hand.

Over the years preceding the Second World War an incessant stream of visitors came—usually on Sunday afternoons—to the house at 10 rue du Parc, Meudon. Some were the members of the Thomist Centers, others personal friends, or foreigners like myself with letters of introduction to Jacques Maritain. There were old and young, students and professors, philosophers, scientists, physicians, writers, poets, musicians. A majority of them were laymen, but there were also priests and religious. The greater number were Catholics, but atheists, Orthodox Christians, Jews, and Protestants came as well.

Many of the writers, painters, and musicians had been drawn to Jacques Maritain by his book *Art and Scholasticism*, first published in 1920. This work surprised them by the understanding it showed of the immediate and concrete problems of artists who were trying to express the spiritual aspirations and anguish of modern man. Aquinas had not written a treatise specifically devoted to aesthetics, but throughout his works were passages, based on Aristotle, concerning art as a product of the intellect and its relationship to reality, the beautiful, and the good. In his book, Jacques collected these scattered passages and combined them with the statements on art by other scholastic philosophers. These theories he then applied to examples of creative work down through the ages and especially to what was going on in painting, music, and poetry in the twentieth century. The relationship between art and morality and the importance of the intention of the artist in treating the problem of evil were among the topics discussed in his book.

Jacques often said that he had Georges Rouault in mind when he began the writing of *Art and Scholasticism*. He had long meditated on the ideas of this revolutionary painter and, in addition, had examined countless work of other contemporary painters and sculptors; he had read much of the creative literature of the day. His familiarity with their work and his respect for the dignity of their vocation were among the qualities that attracted to him so many creative minds.

Besides Rouault, among the painters who passed frequently

through the gate at Meudon were Maurice Denis, Gino Severini, Marc Chagall, Jean Hugo; among the writers, critics, and poets, Julien Green, Henri Ghéon, Robert Valléry-Radot, Max Jacob, and Pierre Reverdy; among the musicians and composers, Georges Auric, Igor Stravinsky, Arthur Lourié, and Nicolas Nabokoff. Many of these attended the meetings of the Thomist Center.

I do not want to give the impression that the meetings of the Center became random discussions of art or that artists were the only ones who came. There were numerous experts in other fields—such as the entomologist W. R. Thompson, the geologist Pierre Termier, the philosophers Gabriel Marcel and Olivier Lacombe, the Orientalist Louis Massignon, the psychiatrist Roland Dalbiez, to mention only a few. All came for the purpose of serious philosophical study and the inspiration it gave them in their work. The programs of the Center always proposed some aspect of Thomistic philosophy and were rigidly adhered to. Other impromptu gatherings of friends—Jacques labeled them "esoteric"—were held at the Maritain home on different Sunday afternoons.

It is not surprising that the study of Saint Thomas and the fervent spiritual lives of the Maritains led to conversions and returns to the Catholic Church. And they themselves believed that the greatest favor they could do their friends was to share with them a faith that meant so much to themselves. The meetings and retreats at Meudon were decisive in many lives. A number of baptisms and professions of faith took place in the little chapel of their home. Jacques was soon following in the footsteps of Léon Bloy as the "omnibus godfather," and Raïssa could soon count as many spiritual children as he—and neither took their duties lightly.

Vocations to the priesthood and to different religious orders were also born at Meudon. Of these there were many, but among the first was that of Prince Vladimir Ghika, of an illustrious Roumanian family, who became a priest and rose high in the ranks of the clergy; of Jacques Froissart, known as Father Bruno of the Carmelite Order, a well-known writer of books on mysticism and editor of *Études Carmélitaines;* of Jean Pierre Altermann, editor of *Vigile;* and of Charles Henrion.

Charles Henrion had known the Maritains since before the First World War. After his conversion, in which Paul Claudel played a role, he had retired to his family home in the Vosges to live a prayerful life and to go about the countryside as a lay preacher. He had fought in the French army during the war, been captured by the Germans, and interned in Switzerland, where he had followed theological courses at the University of Fribourg. His great interest lay in mystical theology, and he and Jacques often met during the years and kept up a lively correspondence. Although undoubtedly qualified, he had not aspired to the priesthood, thinking to live a life of prayer and contemplation in his own way. The Maritains were much attached to him, and seeing the spiritual influence he had over many people, they joined with others in urging Charles Henrion to take holy orders. This he did, but in a manner few had foreseen. He went to North Africa, where he was ordained by the archbishop of Carthage.

Shortly after his ordination, Father Charles left for the desert with another priest, the ex-Admiral Malcor. There they lived in prayer and austerity, and gave medical aid to the Arabs. A third priest joined them, and there was founded at a short distance from their hermitage a community of women, contemplatives like themselves, who looked after the sick and needy among the native women.

Nevertheless Father Charles did not cut entirely his ties with France. For two months each year he came to stay with his mother in the Vosges or with the Maritains at Meudon. With his dark face burned by the desert sun and his glowing eyes, in a white robe emblazoned with a red heart—the garb worn among the Tuaregs by the famous

Charles de Foucauld—he was an impressive figure. Dramatic incidents often occurred during his visits.

One of these was his encounter with the bizarre but undoubted genius Jean Cocteau, a leader of the avant-garde as poet, essayist, novelist, film-maker, and playwright. Some months before this took place, the young musician Georges Auric had brought Cocteau for the first time to 10 rue du Parc, Meudon. Cocteau was in despair over the death of his friend Raymond Radiguet, a promising if eccentric young novelist, and had tried every means to overcome his grief, including the use of opium. For a long time several of his friends had been urging him to return to the practice of his childhood religion, and Auric thought Jacques Maritain could persuade him. That day Jacques had talked to Cocteau at length, and after he left had asked Raïssa to keep the poet in her prayers. For several months Cocteau returned to Meudon for conversations with Jacques, who tried to do everything he could to help him. With Cocteau's doctor and Max Jacob—another poet and a mutual friend—he had discreetly arranged for Cocteau to go to a sanitarium for the cure of his drug habit. This was apparently successful.

On June 15, 1925, a meeting was held at Meudon for the purpose of launching for the publishing firm of Plon a series of books to be called *"Le Roseau d'Or"* (The Golden Reed), with Jacques Maritain as one of the editors. In the small group of prominent writers asked to come to give advice and suggestions was Jean Cocteau. Raïssa, a great admirer of his poetry, was also present at this meeting.

That evening, just as Cocteau was preparing to leave, Father Charles Henrion arrived from the train and came into the room. At the mere sight of his face and white form, Cocteau was hypnotized, falling at once under the spell of the contemplative. Who better could understand a poet's soul? His friends had been telling him for some time that he should see a priest, and here perhaps was one to whom he might turn. Too moved to speak, he did not stay long that evening. On his way out, Raïssa invited him to come to a mass that Father Charles was to say in their chapel on June 19. His reply was evasive.

Two days later Jacques passed by Cocteau's home to urge him not to delay in going to confession to Father Charles, who would not stay much longer in France. Cocteau made no promises but said that he would go to Meudon the following day to *talk* to the priest, and the next day Jacques brought the poet to the arranged meeting. Alone with Father Charles, and after a long talk with him, Cocteau did indeed go to confession. The next morning he came to the Maritains' chapel for mass and received communion with them and several of their intimate friends.

Shortly afterward a book appeared entitled *Letter to Jacques Maritain* in which Cocteau wrote of his experience in extravagant terms. At the first sight of Father Charles, he wrote, he had been made speechless, "groggy, as boxers say, looking through a thick pane at the white object moving in the depth of the sky. I suppose your wife and guests must have noticed; room, books, friends, nothing existed any more. It was then, Maritain, that you pushed me. Pushed me in the back with a blow from your athletic soul, pushed me head first. All saw that I was losing my balance. Nobody came to my rescue, for they knew that to help me then would have been to lose me. Thus I learned of the spirit of this family, one with which Father endows us instantly, and which is not one of the least of the graces of God. A priest gave me the same shock as had Stravinsky and Picasso. . . ."

After this Cocteau often appeared at Meudon to hear mass and to talk with Jacques and Raïssa, impressing everyone by his devout attitude. His return to the sacraments of his religion caused a sensation in Paris, almost a scandal, when at the end of several months, he fell back into his old ways of life. His conversion had been short-lived, to the great unhappiness of the Maritains. Even so, they did not break off this friendship, and Cocteau seems to have kept for them a warm spot in his heart. Years later he was still seeing them and sending them tickets to the openings of his plays. All his efforts were now concentrated on art and the theater. As Pierre Van der Meer charitably remarked forty years later when Cocteau died: "Everything he did, he did with successive sincerities, but with sincerity . . . he was a poet. Even when poets are pagans, they are fixed on beauty, and beauty is a thing of God."

If less spectacular, other conversions under the Maritains' influence were more lasting. Many of those who came into the Church at this time remained fervent Catholics as well as lifelong friends. Among them was Paul Sabon, a gifted surrealist poet, to whom Jacques had communicated his enthusiasm for the works of the Spanish mystic Saint John of the Cross. Sabon's conversion had a strong impact on his future work, although he did not live long enough to realize the full measure of his talents. There was Erik Satie, who gathered around him the much admired group of modern composers known as "The Six." Later there would be Roland Manuel, the music critic, who led to Meudon more friends in the musical world. The Alsatian Baron Alexandre Grunelius and his wife, the former Antoinette Schlumberger, became converts with Jacques and Raïssa as their godparents; I shall say more about them later on, because of the beneficent role the Grunelius family played in the Maritains' lives for over forty years. Willard Hill, a young American businessman in Paris, went to Meudon for a meeting of the Thomist Center, soon became a Catholic, and remained all his life a devoted and helpful friend of the Maritain household.

In speaking of conversions, I should not forget one that touched the Maritains most personally. It was that of Raïssa's mother, Madame Oumansoff. Before his death in 1912, her husband, a believing Jew, had turned to the Catholic faith,

and Raïssa's mother had been greatly troubled and hurt by
this. Although she had great affection for her daughters and
son-in-law and had lived with them since her husband's death,
the subject of religion was like a wall between them. Yet
after twenty years she began, of her own accord, to study
books on Catholicism, and finally asked to be baptized.
Raïssa tells that it made her, Vera, and Jacques "a little
delirious" with joy.

As we know, Raïssa came of Russian-Jewish stock, and of
course could read and speak Russian. Many of her Jewish
friends, as well as others who were Orthodox Christians, were
frequently invited to Meudon. I should mention especially
Nicolas Berdiaeff, philosopher and ideologist, author of such
books as *The End of Our Time* and *The Destiny of Man.*
Early in life he had been a Marxist, but had left the Russian
Social Democratic Party in 1903, abandoning materialism and
atheism for metaphysical and spiritual interests.

Berdiaeff lived at Clamart, about two miles from Meudon,
and his friendship with the Maritains led to an unusual attempt at ecumenism between members of the Roman Catholic
and Orthodox Churches. The Maritains would invite Berdiaeff or some other Russian Orthodox to a gathering to explain
the doctrines and practices of their Church or to comment
on religious conditions in Russia under communism. At Clamart, Berdiaeff conducted similar meetings, and Jacques and
Raïssa attended them, as did various Catholic priests and
Protestant clergymen. The Russians they met there were often
from the Orthodox Divinity Institute in Paris where Berdiaeff
taught, Orthodox priests and nuns, and several Russian-speak-
ing Americans interested in religious affairs in the U.S.S.R.,
among them Donald Lowrie, who later became Berdiaeff's
biographer.

Helen Iswolsky, the daughter of a former Russian minister
of foreign affairs and ambassador to France at the time of the
Bolshevik Revolution, was a member of this group and also

of the Thomist Circle at Meudon. She had remained in Paris with her family after the downfall of the tsars, and as a young girl had followed courses at the Sorbonne, majoring in law and economics. Since then she had made a distinguished reputation as a writer and journalist, dealing especially with social, historical, and religious problems, and was able to contribute a good deal to these discussions.

As I have said, the Maritains tried to confine to Sunday afternoons the reception of visitors and gatherings they held or attended. The rest of the week Jacques devoted to his classes, to other lectures, an enormous correspondence, and work on his books and articles. As always, Raïssa shared his interests, and he would discuss his ideas with her, usually asking her to read over what he had put down. Raïssa was also writing poetry and articles on poetics, and—although she showed them to no one—many notes in her journal and essays on spiritual subjects which were discovered only after her death. On *Art and Scholasticism* she had put in almost as many hours as Jacques, and together they wrote *La Vie d'Oraison* (published in English as *Prayer and Intelligence*), a much admired manual originally intended for the use of the Thomist Centers. From the above books and Jacques's other works published between 1920 and 1926— *Théonas, Antimoderne, Reflections on the Intelligence,* and *Three Reformers: Luther, Descartes, Rousseau*—we can see that they were almost entirely preoccupied with aesthetics, spirituality, and metaphysics at that period.

Any enthusiasm Jacques had professed earlier for socialism had waned since his conversion; politics did not interest him and he had no connection with any political party. Nevertheless, he was surrounded by many Catholics, including priests and theologians he greatly admired, who were members of the royalist and anti-republican movement Action Française, headed by Charles Maurras. Jacques had known Maurras personally and was on friendly if not intimate terms with him, but had never troubled to read his books or to make a serious study of his political or religious ideas. Jacques's awakening was therefore rude when, in 1926, Rome condemned the movement Action Française, the writings of its leaders, and their newspaper, on doctrinal grounds.

V

The Action Française Affair— New Vistas for a Philosopher

Many of the issues in the bitter controversy surrounding the papal condemnation of Action Française have been dead for years—in France as in the Church—but the fallout lingered on for a long time in French politics and in Jacques Maritain's personal life. Everything he wrote during this crisis shows that the decision he felt obliged to make cost him much anguish in the loss of friendships he valued highly; it also led him to turn his philosophical thinking in a new direction.

With his democratic and republican background, Jacques could not have sympathized with the royalist aspirations of Action Française, which advocated the abolition of the republican form of government, a return to the nation's traditional monarchism, and an intransigent nationalism. After the end of the war of 1914, it would have been hard to believe seriously in the restoration to the throne of one of its several claimants, although such an attempt had been made as late as 1873. There were still pockets of pro-royalist sentiment throughout France, as I saw myself when I followed courses at the University of Grenoble in 1926. I then found that Jacques Chevalier, my esteemed professor of philosophy, a devout Catholic and a Bergsonian, was a professed royalist, as were many of the French students and families with whom I associated. At that time I—an American—thought this an amusing provincial anachronism, but soon discovered that such sympathies were quite persistent in other parts of France. Certainly, however, the majority of Jacques's countrymen had come to accept the Third Republic after the revolutionary changes in social and political structures that had taken place over the past century. An exception was the small but activist group of Action Française, still clinging to its ideas of "tradition, order, and patriotism." Actually, its slogan was "Politics Above All," and its activities were based on a stark pragmatism that did not preclude resort to violence.

Charles Maurras, the leader of the movement, was himself an agnostic, but had earlier defended the Catholic Church in its stand against Modernism and in conflicts with the government over anti-clerical laws and the secularization of education. Léon Daudet, a brilliant polemist and journalist, co-editor of the party organ *L'Action Française*, was a practicing Catholic, as were other talented men among those active in the movement, including the historian and journalist Jacques Bainville, and Henri Massis. Many young people, even those in seminaries, followed their lead, as did a number of priests and religious.[1]

Rome itself had been slow to act in the matter of Action Française due to the paradoxical positions taken by its leaders and the makeup of its membership. Although the Church did not in principle favor any particular form of government as against another, the Holy See was alarmed by the growing violence in the activities of Action Française—street demonstrations, student riots, and the like—and especially certain of its underlying ideas. As early as 1914, the Vatican theologians, in response to criticism from certain quarters in France, had drawn up a decree placing on the Index seven writings of Charles Maurras and had included his newspaper in the censure. Pius X agreed that the writings of Maurras brought to his attention were certainly forbidden to Catholics, but the

---

[1] Over the years various members of religious communities who went into exile at the time of the application of the anti-Church Combes laws of 1904 had returned to France; the schools they once conducted had been largely laicized, but priests and religious were again active in charitable and social welfare work.

decree was not published, as he did not want the matter to be brought to a head on the eve of a war he foresaw as inevitable. His successor, Benedict XV, took the same stance, saying that "during war political passions would prevent a just judgement on the part of the Holy See."

In the 1920s, however, the affair took a new turn. Maurras' party was gaining in influence, especially among French intellectuals and the young. Moreover, its leaders became highly critical of the efforts of the Vatican to restore peace with the Third Republic (diplomatic relations had been broken off at the time of the passage of the Combes laws), and launched a violent campaign against international institutions and all those counseling reconciliation between France and Germany. Protests from liberal Catholics, Christian democrats, and supporters of the League of Nations in France led Pope Pius XI personally to reexamine the files.

His study of the writings of Maurras, Daudet, and Bainville convinced him that the matter was not merely political but stemmed from error in underlying principles, namely "positivist naturalism" and "exaggerated nationalism." As for the Church, any admiration Maurras had expressed for it was shown to be based on his concept of it as an institution, a principle of authority, and an organ of discipline. There was no evidence that he recognized its spiritual substance, nor the saving of souls as its primal mission. Pius XI, however, did not resort at once to severe measures. He knew that in the ranks of Action Française were many good Catholics who did not share all of Maurras' views; the Pope thought that they should be warned, and preferably by ecclesiastical authority in their own country.

This warning was given in August 1926 in an open letter to a youth organization from Cardinal Andrieu, archbishop of Bordeaux, in which he strongly advised its members to withdraw from any connection with Action Française as "a danger to the essence of the Christian spirit." When Pope

Pius, in another letter published in the same diocesan paper, approved the cardinal's effort to check the growing influence of Maurras' movement, bitterness grew. *L'Action Française* loudly argued that the condemnation was merely a political measure, that party members must choose between loyalty to the Church and to Action Française.

As Jacques Maritain had never been a member of the party, there was no question of leaving it. But prior to his death in 1917, Father Clérissac, the Maritains' spiritual director, had greatly admired Maurras and approved his movement, which, it should be said, had not yet been revealed in its worst aspects. Later many of those in whom Jacques placed confidence had shared Father Clérissac's opinion. When, in 1920, he and Maurras had finally received Pierre Villard's legacy, Maurras had suggested that each of them turn over a sizable sum to the *Revue Universelle,* an important new periodical for general readership, under the editorship of Jacques Bainville. With his usual generosity and desire to further cultural causes, Jacques had agreed to this, and had later written or edited for the review articles on metaphysical subjects.

However, on the appearance of Cardinal Andrieu's letter and the Pope's reply, Jacques felt that he should make some statement of his personal views. After a study of Maurras' writings, he quickly put out a pamphlet, "An Opinion on Charles Maurras and the Duty of Catholics," in which he examined Maurras' political thinking and pointed out the partial truths it contained as well as its ideological errors. At the same time, he expressed the hope that some clarification would be made and a reconciliation brought about. In this he was swayed by an optimistic belief, held by certain of those around him, that Maurras himself was tending toward conversion to Catholicism. He could not have been more mistaken, for on December 15, 1926, *L'Action Française* published an article refusing submission to the Roman censure and accusing "a little group of simonical agents" of insults to good Frenchmen "in their conscience as believers and to their honor as men."

In a Consistory five days later Pius XI replied with a formal prohibition to all Catholics to belong to a movement or to read the journal "of men whose writings are in opposition to our dogmas and our morality." On December 29, 1926, the decree which the Holy Office had drawn up in 1914 against Maurras' writings was published, and to it was added a specific condemnation of the journal he directed because of articles by himself, Daudet, and others.

The storm broke. Not since the Dreyfus affair had there been such a division of opinions and loyalties in France. This extended into the ranks of the hierarchy, and priests, religious, and even a French cardinal in the Curia openly expressed their sympathy for the condemned organization. With a few exceptions, the papal measure was defended only with luke-warmness in the French Catholic press. Immediately Maurras and his supporters launched an attack of unprecedented violence against the Pope, and *L'Action Française* became the most anti-clerical paper in France. For practicing Catholics in the ranks of the movement, a painful choice had to be made; families were divided and friendships brought to an end as many rebelled and left the Church; the submission of certain others was only nominal.

Jacques Maritain never had any doubt as to where his allegiance lay. Yet he bitterly reproached himself for not examining the fundamental principles of Action Française and detecting the errors at the base of its activities. He forthwith severed any connection with those who continued to adhere to the movement, fully realizing what this would cost him in the loss of friends and followers, including the young royalists (*camelots du roi*) who had flocked to his lectures at the Institut Catholique.

He now began the writing of *La Primauté du Spirituel*

(English translation titled *The Things That Are Not Cae-sar's*), published in 1927. In this he first examined the theologi-cal and evangelical principles distinguishing spiritual power and temporal power that regulated the relationship of Church and State; secondly, he applied this to the crisis of con-science faced by Catholics because of membership in Action Française, showing toward them fraternal charity and under-standing in the ordeal they were going through. In addition, he attempted to discern in broad outline the general directions that "integral Christian politics" should take under conditions in a world which he recognized as certainly far from ideal. Of this time he later wrote: "There then began for me a period of reflection devoted to moral and political philosophy, in which I tried to work out the character of authentically Christian politics and to establish, in the light of a philosophy of history and culture, the true significance of democratic inspiration and the nature of the new humanism for which we are waiting."

The disastrous division caused by the Action Française controversy continued for some ten years, and the results even longer in Jacques Maritain's career, for not only had he lost friends but he had created enemies. It is true that the papal condemnation was lifted in 1937 when Maurras—who had lost many followers and subscribers to *L'Action Française*—expressed to Pope Pius XII his regret for what had been "dis-respectful, injurious, and even unjust" in the attitude of Ac-tion Française and "rejected any principle and any theory contrary to the teaching of the Church." This, however, does not seem to have greatly changed his ideological judgments, for in his writings thereafter he supported Mussolini in Italy and Primo de Rivera in Spain, and after the Second World War was imprisoned by France for collaboration with the Germans. As we shall see, during this time Jacques Maritain's thinking and activities were cast in a quite different direction.

I mentioned above the enemies Jacques made by the position

he took in the Action Française affair and by his book *La
Primauté du Spirituel.* Among these, of course, were the
leaders of the movement, whose animosity followed him
for many a year. More personally devastating to him was the
loss of his close friend Henri Massis, who accused him of
betraying his philosophical vocation by interfering in a purely
political matter. Dom Delatte, the abbot of Solesmes, who
had been the Maritains' friend since the days of Heidelberg,
had so admired Action Française that he broke harshly with
Jacques. Even Father Garrigou-Lagrange, a man of the Right
who was torn apart by the crisis although he did not refuse
to obey the Church, was decidedly cool for a time. However,
except for the first year after the appearance of Jacques's
book, he continued to come to Meudon to preach retreats
and advise on many matters. For his part, Jacques said: "I
only want to say that our differences in political matters
never diminished the affection that Raïssa and I had for him."[2]

Jacques was less concerned with the reaction of those who
did not know him and who misinterpreted his views, accusing
him of blind subservience to the Church. He had decided
that his future as a philosopher should be a personal venture
and that he should take the risk of being misunderstood so
long as he followed his conscience as a Christian. He did not
want to act politically, but to apply to the field of social
and political action the teachings he held to be logical ex-
tensions of the thought of Thomas Aquinas.

Jacques saw about him the de-Christianization of the masses
in postwar France. Although there was in existence a Catholic
social movement which based its ideas on the encyclicals of
the Popes, he felt that too few Catholics had played a part in
the efforts to effect a real improvement in the condition of
the workers. Forty years before, in *Rerum novarum,* Leo
XIII had denounced atheistic communism but at the same time
the abuses of capitalism, and had stressed the necessity of

---

[2] *Carnet de Notes,* p. 231.

economic justice for workers and attention to their temporal welfare. With a few notable exceptions, this had not brought about changes in the ways and thinking of the majority of Jacques's compatriots and co-religionists. However, with the appearance of the more specific *Quadragesimo anno* of Pius XI in 1931, new impetus was given to the promotion of Christian social justice. Jacques now identified himself with the leaders of this growing movement and especially those who were trying to spread its doctrinal base by means of the press.

Several religious Orders had already turned their attention to this medium. The Jesuits had started the *Cahiers Populaires*, a periodical concerned with action among workers; a number of their prominent scholars and theologians were studying and writing on problems allied to communism, as were also a group of Carmelites. But it was especially the Dominican Order which was active in this direction. A small community of its younger members on the Paris avenue of Latour Maubourg was issuing periodicals and books in the spiritual, cultural, and social areas under the imprint of the publishing firm Le Cerf. In 1928, when Father Garrigou-Lagrange did not come to give the retreat of the Thomist Center, it was preached by Father Bernadot, the head of the Latour Maubourg community, editor of *La Vie Intellectuelle* and later of *Sept*, a weekly founded in 1934 to give a liberal Christian viewpoint on current events. After that Father Bernadot frequently attended the meetings at Meudon, bringing with him some of his co-workers, and Jacques's name often appeared over articles in the publications of the Dominicans of Le Cerf.

Still it was among laymen that Jacques was most anxious to extend his efforts. He therefore interested himself in the foundation and practical arrangements for publication of the review *Esprit*. The youthful founder and editor of this monthly was Emmanuel Mounier, who met Jacques Maritain in 1928 when he came to one of the gatherings held at Meudon. At that time he and two collaborators were preparing a book on Charles Péguy, whose writings had largely influenced Mounier's thinking. When this manuscript was ready, Jacques read it, made suggestions, and included the book in his collection, *"Roseau d'Or."* The next year Mounier approached him with the idea of a review which he and his friend Georges Izard were talking of starting. It was to deal with literature, art, philosophy, and political questions. Although it would have no ecclesiastical connection, it would seek to develop Maritain's and Berdiaeff's ideas of Christian humanism. Jacques encouraged Mounier in this undertaking, and aided him in his search for a publisher and contributors.

Esprit became more than a review. It was a movement based on Mounier's theory of "personalism," an ideological framework for a just balance between man and society. Mounier and his staff had little money, but unstintingly gave of themselves, and had as their headquarters two dingy rooms in the Gare du Nord. Although never large, the movement held "congresses" of young people and managed to acquire representatives in almost every city and town in France. As its leaders wanted to make their influence international, representatives from other countries were appointed to attend their meetings; among these were the Spanish historian Alfredo Mendizábel and also Gouverneur Paulding, a former member of the staff of *The Commonweal,* an influential American weekly edited by Catholic laymen.

For the ten years preceding the Second World War, Jacques Maritain never lost his interest in *Esprit* and in Emmanuel Mounier personally. He saw Mounier constantly and tried to advise him, although the editor of *Esprit* guarded his independence and did not adopt all of Jacques's views. Jacques was concerned above all with the primacy of spiritual considerations, whereas Mounier was inclined to take somewhat revolutionary political positions.

With Jacques's enormous capacity for work, his interests in the field of journalism do not seem to have slowed down the writing of his books. In the first half of the 1930s were published such important works of his as *Religion and Culture* (1931), *The Degrees of Knowledge* (1932), *Freedom in the Modern World* (1933), *A Preface to Metaphysics* (1934), *The Frontiers of Poetry* (1935), the last a continuation of his thinking in *Art and Scholasticism*. In addition, he began to play a role in bringing before the French-speaking public the work of other writers in France and foreign countries. These books were included (in translation where necessary) in a series of books he edited for the publishing firm of Desclée de Brouwer.

In 1929, to the rejoicing of the Maritains, the Van der Meers had returned from Holland to live in Paris. The intimate relationship of the two families continued, and Jacques Maritain and Pierre Van der Meer worked together on the publishing ventures at Desclée. Pierre was now director of the Paris branch of this Belgian firm, and after he took over its management, three collections were started: *"Les Îles,"* *"Questions Disputées,"* and *"Bibliothèque Française de Philosophie."* Jacques was appointed as general editor of the first two, and for the philosophical series he was co-editor with Abbé Charles Journet of the University of Fribourg.

Pierre Van der Meer worked closely with Jacques on these series until 1933, when as the result of a great loss there came about a drastic change in his life. His son Pierre-Léon (Pieterke) died at the Benedictine monastery of Oosterhout at the age of thirty. The young man had carried out his childhood intention to become a Benedictine and a priest and for some years had been an exemplary religious. His sister Anne-Marie had later joined a convent of Benedictine nuns at Oosterhout. Each summer Pierre and Christine had gone to Holland to spend at least a part of their vacations near their children. Following their son's untimely death, his grief-stricken parents came to what Raïssa, who knew of their great love for one another, called "a fearful resolution." It was to separate and to become religious themselves. (To Him who had taken away their cloak, they would give their coat also.)

After persisting in their decision for the year specified by their spiritual advisers, the Van der Meers disposed of all their possessions. Pierre took Christine to Solesmes to enter a Benedictine convent, then went to the abbey of Oosterhout to replace his son. For over eighteen months the two lived on the surface as fervent members of their communities; within themselves they were going through untold agony. When the time came for Pierre to take his vows in the Benedictine Order, his abbot journeyed to Solesmes to see Christine, wishing to be reassured of the reality of their vocations. There for the first time he learned from letters that Christine showed him of the couple's mutual suffering. Saying that they could not go on living in such a way, he told them to return to the world in peace.

Very soon Pierre came from Holland and Christine from Solesmes to meet at the Maritains' house at Meudon. Jacques and Raïssa always spoke of this reunion with emotion. Before long the Van der Meers found a new home for themselves not far away, and within a few weeks Pierre was back at his old desk at Desclée de Brouwer. Once again Christine had a garden to work in and could go back to the painting and designing in which she excelled. Before Christine died, she and Pierre were to have almost twenty more years of life together.

While Pierre Van der Meer was at Oosterhout, his work at Desclée was taken over by Stanislas Fumet, an able young writer and editor, who had known the Maritains since his demobilization from the army after the First World War. He and Jacques had met at the Café Rotonde, near the Montparnasse station, where Jacques often went with his friends when his classes were over and before taking the train to Versailles. The two men were first drawn to one another by an interest in art; soon Fumet, his wife Anouïta, and her brother were attending the meetings of the Thomist Center at Meudon. Stanislas Fumet and Jacques had also been associated as co-editors of the *"Roseau d'Or"* series. The appointment of one so congenial as successor to Pierre Van der Meer was a great relief to Jacques, for he knew they could work together. After Pierre's return from the monastery, Fumet retained his connection with Desclée for some years, and he and Jacques were to be united in this and numerous other communities of interest.

Of the French publishing firms with which Jacques was associated at various times, either as editor or author, it can be said that his closest—and longest—connection was with Desclée de Brouwer. As editor of the series for them, his desk was piled high with manuscripts to be read; he prepared reports on them and wrote letters to the authors. In all this the faithful Vera acted as his secretary, typing his own manuscripts and correspondence, making appointments, defending him against unwanted intrusions. And throughout this time, Jacques and Raïssa kept up their contacts with poets, musicians, and artists, going when possible to expositions and concerts of those among their friends, Jacques taught his classes at the Institut Catholique and frequently met with discussion groups, large and small.

In January of 1931, he was asked to read a paper on "The Cartesian Heritage" at the Franco-Russian Studio in Paris, and it was followed by an acrimonious debate. As he had stated earlier in his book *Three Reformers*, he regarded the philosophy of the seventeenth-century thinker as "the great French sin in the history of modern thought" in its purely idealistic concept of knowledge ("angelism") and its separation of the various branches of wisdom from one another. Honored in France as the father of modern philosophy,

Descartes is regarded almost as a national hero. Maritain's dissent was attacked by certain Russian philosophers, French professors, and journalists, all proclaiming themselves advocates of "humanism." On the basis of Aquinas' link between thought and reality, and his synthesis of the different disciplines of knowledge, Jacques defended his ideas with eloquence and sincerity. He seems to have emerged victorious from the fray, a verbatim report of which is given in the *Cahiers de la Quinzaine*. In any case, he lost no time in putting together *The Dream of Descartes*, a book published the following year.

The Maritains regarded the ecumenical aspect of the meetings at Clamart as very important and attended them whenever they could. Sometimes lively debates on metaphysical matters took place between Nicolas Berdiaeff and Jacques Maritain when the former's Eastern mysticism and Jacques's strict Thomism led them to disagree—but always with courtesy and friendliness. On social questions they saw eye to eye, and the solutions they proposed were practically the same in their defense of the human person against bondage to things and to materialistic economic and social values. The two philosophers continued their friendly meetings and discussions until the separation caused by war.

Besides his activities in and around Paris, Jacques traveled frequently to fill lecture engagements outside France; for instance, within a few months in the fall of 1931, he gave a lecture in Geneva, three in Milan, one in Louvain, and six in Salzburg. Returning from the Austrian trip, he stopped for a week of well-earned rest with Nicolas Nabokoff, a frequent visitor to Meudon, who was spending his own vacation in Alsace. The young composer met Jacques at the railway station in Strasbourg, and with him was a friend: the Baron Alexandre Grunelius. Jacques was immediately invited to the Grunelius château in the nearby village of Kolbsheim, and was welcomed by the other members of the family. Within a few months after this first meeting, Alexandre and Antoinette Grunelius came to Meudon, and so began an intimate and affectionate association that was to last for many years. As I mentioned earlier, when the Gruneliuses became Catholics, the Maritains were their godparents. For many summers, both before and after the Second World War, Jacques, Raïssa, and Vera spent a part of their vacations at Kolbsheim, where a guest house was turned over to them and every provision made for their comfort and privacy. They came to regard it as a second home—and in a sad sense Kolbsheim was to become their last earthly resting place.

Earlier in 1931, Jacques had found another ally in the person of Étienne Gilson, the distinguished historian of medieval philosophy, who had risen to support him at one of the Clamart meetings in a difference of opinion with others present as to the Thomistic relationship between philosophy and faith. From that time on the two Catholic philosophers were frequently in consultation, and their names are associated as the leaders of modern Thomistic teaching. Dr. Gilson was then giving courses at the Sorbonne, lecturing in other European universities and in the United States at Harvard. He had contributed to the founding, in 1929, of the Institute of Medieval Studies at Saint Michael's College, an affiliate of the University of Toronto; each year since he had gone there to lecture. Not long after his meeting with Étienne Gilson, Jacques received an invitation to give a course at the Institute of Medieval Studies in the winter of 1932–33. This invitation to Canada turned his attention to possibilities for the spread of Thomism in another continent, and he decided to investigate them.

Before telling of his initial American experiences in the following pages, I should like to explain how I came to know Jacques and Raïssa Maritain. Here I must retrace my steps a little, for I met them a few months before Jacques set out on the first of what were to be his many transatlantic journeys.

VI

A Thomist in America

My first meeting with the Maritains was almost by accident, and happened in a roundabout way. I had gone to Paris in August 1931 as editorial secretary of the newly organized French Book Club, a small corporation started by my brother Thomas Kernan and myself. Its purpose was the distribution in America of works in the French language along the lines of the book-of-the-month clubs then springing into existence. The monthly selections were to be made by a committee of judges in Paris, knowledgeable in literary matters and with some idea of American tastes and preferences. For this purpose I was armed with a number of letters to prominent writers and critics by Paul Claudel, then ambassador of France to Washington.

In his bluff way, Ambassador Claudel had greatly encouraged our undertaking, and when I went to see him had made suggestions as to the membership of the committee of judges to be formed. In fact, he had given me more letters of introduction than I needed, in case the first four personages approached did not accept. This did not happen, and a committee was quickly set up consisting of André Maurois; Countess Aldebert de Chambrun, the former Clara Longworth; Abbé Ernest Dimnet, author of *The Art of Thinking;* and Firmin Roz, an able critic and director of the Canadian House at the University City in Paris.

Although he knew the philosopher well, Ambassador Claudel did not give me a letter to Jacques Maritain, nor did I think to ask for it, since our readers were expected to be a French-reading public wanting such current books as novels, biography, history. However, just as I was leaving New York,

Michael Williams, editor of *The Commonweal*, with whom I had been working on several projects, put in my hands a letter of introduction to Jacques Maritain.

My work for the French Book Club consisted in making contacts with French publishing houses in order to find out in advance what titles they were bringing out, getting galleys or page proofs, and submitting them to the judges for possible selection. After they had reached a decision, I had to come to terms with the publisher for a special printing, give the purchase order, and see that the books were delivered to the packers for shipment to New York. Setting up this routine for what was soon three thousand books monthly (for our New York office had been active in securing subscriptions) required quite a bit of doing, and it was some time before I could settle down in my small office in the American Library, at that time on the rue de l'Elysée, close to the American Embassy.

Some eight months went by, and although I had met many writers, publishers, and editors, I had not sent my letter of introduction to Jacques Maritain. In fact, so much time had elapsed that I hesitated to do so. We were finally brought together by a neighbor on the rue de Bourgogne, where I lived. This was the music critic Roland Manuel, a stocky, pleasant-faced man, who told me that he was a godson of Jacques Maritain's. When he learned that I had a letter of introduction to the philosopher but felt too much time had gone by to present it, he said I surely must do so, and that he himself would arrange for me to go to Meudon.

Within a few days, I found a note from Roland Manuel at my door to the effect that the Maritains would be glad to see me one evening the following week, but that if I could be present at a study session the intervening Sunday to come by all means and "without prejudice to the evening engagement." Roland Manuel added that he was not sure he would be free that Sunday to go with me, but enclosed a rough map he had drawn of Meudon and the way to reach 10 rue du Parc from the train. I still have his note and the little map, for it showed the way to a home where began a friendship that was to be for me a source of inspiration for over forty years.

As I had to leave on a business trip, I was unable to go to Meudon on the two days suggested, but on my return a few weeks later I had another invitation. This time Roland Manuel could accompany me. I met him on a Sunday afternoon on the platform of the Invalides station, and with him a Roumanian musician whose name I forget. I do remember that all the way out on the train the two gentlemen discussed with great animation "the aesthetics of the baroque," and I grew more and more depressed, fearing that I was heading into some very deep waters.

However, after the climb up the hill to the Maritains' villa, I was reassured by Vera's amiable welcome at the door. She led us into a modestly furnished room with blue-gray walls on which hung a painting by Rouault and another by Severini. On the mantelpiece were pictures of Léon Bloy, Saint Thomas Aquinas, Ernest Psichari.

As many guests had already arrived and were engaged in earnest conversation, I was somewhat confused until suddenly Raïssa came to sit beside me. As yet Jacques was not visible, but I noticed that one at a time someone present would rise to go through a door leading into the next room—which was Jacques's study—and, on emerging, be succeeded by another. Raïssa explained that these were friends who had some personal matter to discuss, and said that Jacques would be in shortly; she added that this was not one of their regular study sessions, but an impromptu gathering of friends. She then introduced me to a number of those around us, including Pierre Van der Meer and Emmanuel Mounier. Among the others, I recall Henri Ghéon, Ernest Psichari's sister Henriette, Willard Hill, and Jacques's niece Éveline Garnier, his sister Jeanne's daughter.

My first impressions of Jacques and Raïssa are still vivid. A few months before, Raïssa's mother had died, and she had been deeply affected. In her black dress, she seemed very frail and almost wraithlike except for the youthful, clear voice and expressive eyes. When Jacques appeared, he came over to us and I found myself before a man of immense kindliness who inspired confidence at once. His look was so honest and good, his welcome so cordial that the rather forbidding picture I had formed of the philosopher was immediately dispelled. I was surprised that, in spite of the presence of so many others, he placed me at once. He spoke of Michael Williams' letter and asked about my work in Paris, listening to my answers with the attention of one who has accepted another as a friend. That day I had no further chance to exchange more than a few words with him, but I soon came to know him better, for he and Raïssa were cordial in saying as I left that I must come again.

After that first meeting, I was invited frequently to Meudon and met a number of the Maritains' friends. Henri Ghéon was kind enough to suggest in advance that I be with them when he read at Meudon the delightful "miracle plays" on which he was working; occasionally he came into my office in Paris to discuss his book projects. The painter Maurice Denis took me to expositions of his work and that of other artists.

I came to know Nicolas Berdiaeff rather well. I never went to Clamart, but saw him on various occasions at Meudon. When Michael Williams came to Paris, he asked me to arrange a meeting with the Russian philosopher, and Berdiaeff came into the city, where the two had a long conversation at 10 rue de l'Elysée. As Michael Williams spoke neither French nor Russian, nor Berdiaeff English, I acted as interpreter. This was somewhat difficult because, in addition to the complexity of the ideas they discussed, Berdiaeff had a speech impediment, a tic that caused his jaw to lock, so there were alarming pauses in the conversation. A few months later, however, an article by him along the lines that he and Michael Williams had discussed that day appeared in *The Commonweal.*

Willard Hill showed me many courtesies. I grew very fond of this precise, bespectacled compatriot who worked at the International Chamber of Commerce and looked and spoke like a Harvard professor. I saw him frequently in Paris, for he lived nearby, and later in New York when he came to this country on a visit. His attachment to the Maritains was matched by his love for France. He could not imagine living anywhere else, and managed to remain even during the Second World War in the home of a friend in a remote district of the Unoccupied Zone. He later formed ties with the Little Brothers of Jesus, a religious community inspired by Charles de Foucauld, and worked for a number of years in connection with its publications.

Willard was at Meudon when, in 1932, I attended several sessions of the retreat of the Thomist Center. That year, exceptionally, it was conducted by the Dominican theologian Father Sertillanges. There were at least 150 retreatants, among them Richard O'Sullivan, who headed a Thomist society in England, Donald Woodruff, editor of the London *Tablet,* the Van der Meers, the psychiatrist Roland Dalbiez. The religious services were devoutly attended; Father Sertillanges, radiant in his white habit, was an impressive speaker, and talked to the assembly twice a day. In between, Jacques and Vera moved from group to group, attentive to everyone's needs. Raïssa appeared only briefly for the instructions, obviously being very ill at the time.

By the end of December, her health had improved and she insisted that Jacques leave for Toronto to give his first course at the Institute of Medieval Studies. From all reports, he was enthusiastically received by the faculty and students of an institution where his writings were held in high esteem. And that year at Toronto began his long friendship and collaboration with Dr. Gerald Phelan, the Institute's director of studies who, with Dr. Gilson and the Basilian Fathers, had been one of the founders of the Institute.

After graduate studies in Canada and the United States, Dr. Phelan had his Ph.D. from Louvain and had worked in the psychological laboratories there and at the universities of Cambridge, England, and Würzburg, Germany. So he and Jacques had many grounds in common. Dr. Phelan was to become one of the ablest American exponents of Jacques Maritain's thought and authored the first book in English on his philosophy. In this he said that he regarded Jacques "as *The Philosopher* of the twentieth century, a God-given guide and leader of thought for the age we claim as ours."

Jacques remained in the scholarly atmosphere of the Institute of Medieval Studies until the end of his courses. He then went to Chicago, as he had accepted an invitation to give a lecture on "Culture and Liberty" at the university of that city.

Under its young president, Robert Hutchins, the university enjoyed a high academic rating; on its faculty were men of wide reputation in almost every field. As much as he appreciated their achievements and the recognition they received in the scholarly world, President Hutchins considered that an over-all view was lacking—as in American education in general—of the interdependence of the various branches of knowledge, and that some measure of unity in regard to permanent values should be sought. His own reading in philosophy had convinced him that the problems of existence as set forth by Greek and medieval thinkers were as important as they had ever been. He had written: "If we can revitalize metaphysics and restore it to its place in the higher learning,

OUR FRIEND, JACQUES MARITAIN
90

we may be able to establish rational order in the modern
world as well as in the universities."

In revising curricula to cut across departmental lines and
to discover general principles from which all might benefit,
President Hutchins was opposed by various faculty members
and especially those of the philosophy department. These
upheld the positivist and pragmatic approach to philosophy
and distrusted anything "medieval." However, Hutchins had
succeeded in attracting from Columbia University the Thomist scholar Mortimer Adler, who was teaching Thomist ethics
not in the philosophy department but in the law school, and
Adler's courses were being followed by a number of students
from other faculties.

Robert Hutchins regarded Jacques Maritain as the leading
exponent of Thomist philosophy. The original French edition of Jacques's *Degrees of Knowledge* had been recently
published (1932) and was being widely discussed in intellectual circles. In inviting him to Chicago as a visiting lecturer,
Hutchins had hopes that he might eventually be installed as a
member of the faculty of philosophy. This did not happen, although Jacques was to return to the university a number of
times to speak under other sponsorship.

During his first visit to Chicago, he was the guest of Dr.
and Mrs. Frank Lillie. Dr. Lillie headed the division of biological sciences at the university, and he and his wife, Frances
Crane Lillie, arranged for Jacques to meet a number of personages in artistic and intellectual circles in addition to Dr.
Lillie's colleagues at the university. Among the latter, Jacques
began his association with Mortimer Adler, who, although
he did not share Jacques's religious beliefs, was already recognized as the leading American Neo-Thomist. He helped
Jacques in his early struggles to put his lectures—and later
several books, notably *Scholasticism and Politics*—into English, and they were associated later in various philosophical
and cultural ventures. It was with such men at Chicago as

Mortimer Adler, Robert Hutchins, John Nef, and Stringfellow Barr that Jacques was to discuss his preoccupations with the problems of democracy and considerably to develop his own views.

Mrs. Frank Lillie—a convert to Catholicism—had borne the expenses of Jacques's first visit to Chicago and paid for the publication of his lecture. She sent a copy of this to two friends, Dr. and Mrs. John U. Nef, who were away from the city at the time. Dr. Nef, a professor in the economics department, had long shared President Hutchins' opinions regarding the limitations of academic specialization and the desirability of a freer exchange of ideas among professors and students. His great personal interest was in contemporary art, examples of which he and his wife had been collecting since some years of residence in Europe in the 1920s. Elinor Nef was a woman of great taste, an accomplished writer and scholar.

In his recent book *Search for Meaning* (1973), Dr. Nef tells that he and Mrs. Nef were impressed by Jacques's lecture on liberty, and when in the summer of 1933 they went to France, they carried a letter of introduction to Jacques Maritain from Mrs. Lillie. Unfortunately, when they reached Paris, Jacques was away. Raïssa, however, replied with the suggestion that they come to Meudon to meet Vera and herself. When, in the course of conversation, Dr. Nef said that he had hoped Jacques might be persuaded to return to Chicago, Raïssa intimated that she knew her husband would be interested in an appointment to the university on a part-time basis. Dr. Nef let Robert Hutchins know of this, and after he went back to Chicago, the two worked together in trying to secure Jacques's appointment to the philosophy department. They were not successful, but other lecture arrangements were made, and in the fall of 1934, Jacques returned to the university. Again he was the guest of the Lillies, but after that, whenever he went to Chicago, he stayed at the home of the Nefs.

In John Nef, Jacques Maritain had found a very warm personal friend. They had the same aesthetic preoccupations and comprehension of the artistic temperament and motivation. They shared the same interest in educational reform. Even though they differed in religious and certain philosophical areas, Jacques felt that he could talk freely to this friend and often turned to him for advice on practical matters. Aware of Jacques's personal situation, Dr. Nef smoothed his path in many thoughtful and generous ways. To the end of his life Jacques spoke of John Nef with gratitude and affection and dedicated to him several of his important books.

In 1938 and again in 1940, Raïssa and Vera came with Jacques to the United States, and when in Chicago the three stayed at the Nef apartment, sharing an appreciation of music, art, and the theater. Their hosts' pictures were an inexhaustible subject of interest and conversation, especially as among them were works by Rouault and Chagall, the Maritains' friends.

For some years preceding the Second World War, Dr. Nef worked for the formation of an interdepartmental structure that would encourage students and instructors to carry on their special work in a context that promoted the discovery of relationships rather than disparities between disciplines. His efforts came to fruition in 1942 when The Committee on Social Thought was formally inaugurated at the university. This group brought many famous scholars, writers, and artists to lecture at Chicago. One of those who would be most frequently invited was Jacques Maritain, and Raïssa sometimes accompanied him.

The other Midwestern university with which Jacques first established connections in the early 1930s was Notre Dame. Its president, Father John O'Hara (who later became cardinal-archbishop of Philadelphia), was also trying to bring about a

A Thomist in America   93

creative synthesis between the varying branches of knowledge, and invited distinguished writers and artists to speak at the university he headed.

Among those appointed to teaching posts at Notre Dame were two friends of Jacques's. Yves Simon, a former pupil at the Institut Catholique, later a lecturer in philosophy there and at the Catholic University of Lille, joined Notre Dame's philosophy department in 1938. Already installed as associate professor of politics was the Russian-born Waldemar Gurian, a convert from Judaism to Catholicism. A strong opponent of communism, he had studied law, sociology, and philosophy in Germany, and was editor of an important newspaper in Cologne when he was forced to leave in 1934. After that he had edited in Switzerland a weekly paper "devoted exclusively to the philosophical and sociopolitical analysis of Nazism." Gurian often acknowledged his debt to the writings of Maritain and Berdiaeff, both of whom he had known in Paris.

Following a meeting in 1938 with Waldemar Gurian at the Nef apartment, Jacques was invited to preside at a symposium on social and political philosophy at Notre Dame after he had finished his lectures that year at the University of Chicago. This was at a time when many American Catholics and large sectors of the Catholic press were highly critical of the anti-Franco stand Jacques had taken on the Spanish Civil War (about this more in my next chapter). To many people at that time his position smacked of heresy. Although he had explained this position in a written statement sent prior to his going to South Bend, and despite the warmth of his introduction to the assembly by Father Leo R. Ward of the philosophy department, he was besieged with questions.

Raïssa and Vera were with him, and according to reports this was not an entirely comfortable visit, for there was no guest house on the campus and the three were housed in the student hospital, where a slight atmosphere of suspicion regarding their orthodoxy surrounded them because they did not side with Franco, whose cause was favored by the majority of American Catholics at that time. In addition, there was no working space provided for study or writing, and during their stay the trustees of the university arrived for a meeting and the Maritains had to give up their quarters. This proved a blessing, for they were received with open arms by Sister Madeleva, the president of Saint Mary's College across the road from the university. I had known this remarkable nun, a gifted poet, in Oxford, London, and Paris. On a visit I made to her shortly after the Maritains left, she regaled me with an account of their stay and spoke of the pleasure it had been for everyone at Saint Mary's College, especially as their visit had coincided with that of their old friends Charles du Bos and his wife.

Although Jacques's first visit to Notre Dame took place under rather awkward circumstances, the university more than made up subsequently for the coolness some had initially displayed. He was invited back repeatedly, and his association with the university became even closer when Dr. Gerald Phelan left Toronto in 1946 to found the Medieval Institute at Notre Dame and to head its department of philosophy. For a long time Jacques lectured at Notre Dame once and sometimes twice a year, and for a while he was visiting professor. In 1958, he was honored by the establishment of the Maritain Center under Father Leo R. Ward and Dr. Joseph Evans. The Center houses several thousand books—on or by Jacques Maritain and a number of annotated volumes from his personal library—and many of his manuscripts and letters. The members of the Center have been active in translating his works, in compiling anthologies of them on related subjects, and in publishing essays on different aspects of his thought.

Even if it can be said that it was in the Middle West that

Maritain "first met America in the flesh," he was soon to make his way to the eastern part of the United States. Here I must go back to an afternoon in 1933 when, as I was leaving 10 rue du Parc, Jacques came to the door and went out with me through the garden. As we leaned on the parapet, before us the panoramic view of Paris' domes and steeples, we had a long talk. Among other things he spoke of his trips to Toronto, Chicago, and Notre Dame, and said that he would like in the future to lecture in or around New York, although at the moment he did not know just when he would be free to do so. I told him I was certain that in literary and university circles in the East there would be many people eager to hear him, and that perhaps I could help with the arrangements. The outcome was that the plans we discussed that afternoon were put in motion the following year after I left Paris to work in the New York office of the French Book Club. The Catholic Book Club, of which my brother was president, agreed to sponsor Jacques's lecture. So great was the advance interest that it was decided to hold it in Town Hall. Jacques spoke there on the afternoon of November 5, 1934; his subject was "Knowledge and Wisdom," an application of the philosophy of Aquinas to modern problems of art and science.

Among the notables present on that occasion were the presidents of Columbia, Princeton, Fordham, and the chancellor of New York University. The big hall was filled to overflowing with professors, students, clergy, and readers of Jacques's books. Daniel Sargent, who taught at Harvard and had been introduced to scholastic philosophy and to Jacques while in France some years before, came down from Boston to offer his help. As Jacques was concerned at having to give his speech in English, Daniel Sargent and I sat that morning in the empty auditorium listening to him rehearse it. That afternoon he did indeed speak with a strong accent, but the audience seemed enthusiastic and afterward he was overwhelmed by those who wanted to talk to him personally. The same evening, Dr. Nicholas Murray Butler, the president of Columbia, gave a dinner in his honor, attended by a mixed group of socialites and other prominent New Yorkers. My brother, who accompanied him, said he feared Jacques had been too exhausted to enjoy it.

Immediately following the Town Hall lecture, Jacques had invitations to address other audiences, but he did not like extemporaneous speaking and felt that his stay was too brief to give him time to prepare another lecture. One invitation for an informal discussion, however, he did accept. It came from Peter Maurin, a voluble Frenchman in workmen's clothes who asked him to come to the House of Hospitality of the Catholic Worker on East Fifteenth Street to meet Dorothy Day and other members of their group. Through the antennae which he seemed to have in all directions, Jacques already knew of their work.

Dorothy Day was a convert from Marxism to Catholicism. With Peter Maurin's help, she had started the Catholic Worker movement the year before, in 1933, at the height of the Depression. She and her co-workers lived in voluntary poverty, relying only on charitable contributions, and gave what they had without question to those who came to them for shelter, food—and hope. The long bread lines that gathered each day before their door were mute testimony to the need for their existence. Similar Houses of Hospitality were being opened by them in other cities, where, despite meager means, the same aid was given to the poor and unfortunate. Dorothy, an able editor and writer who had worked on a number of papers, also undertook with the help of her staff the publishing of a monthly paper, *The Catholic Worker*, to create interest in their work and to advocate social justice and pacifism. They had quoted Jacques Maritain's writings frequently.

When, a few days after his Town Hall lecture, Jacques went down to the Lower East Side, he found a large crowd

1. and 2. Jacques Maritain and Raïssa Maritain at the time of their marriage

3. Ernest Psichari (Harlingue-Viollet)

4. Charles Péguy (Harlingue-Viollet)

5. Léon Bloy (Photo Viollet)

6. Stanislas Fumet (Lipnitzki-Viollet)

GREAT FRIENDS OF EARLY DAYS

7. Jacques Maritain at the Sorbonne, age 16

8. At Meudon, 1932

9. Vera Oumansoff in New York

10. Raïssa Maritain, 1944

11. Ambassador of France to the Vatican (Photo Viollet)

12. Lecturing at Princeton (Photo Mottar)

13. In the Jardin des Plantes, January 1973 (Photo Boudinet)

14. Coffin of Jacques Maritain in chapel of the Little Brothers of Jesus at Toulouse (Photo Yan)

assembled at the Catholic Worker, in fact more than the place would hold, so that many were standing outside the open door. He tried to talk to as many as he could, then took part in a discussion of the "pluralist State" concerning which he was asked many questions. His explanation of it was a "federation" of diverse juridical structures with a moral unity of orientation that would deserve the name of Christian. "It would be polarized through the knowledge of the spiritual dignity of the human person and of the love which is due him."[1] On this occasion Jacques spoke in French—translated by Peter Maurin as they went along—and told them of his admiration for a work that showed "so much good will, such courage, such generosity."

While Jacques was still in New York, the Catholic Book Club was also able to arrange for him to repeat his Town Hall lecture at the Catholic University in Washington. It was his first visit there and my brother Tom went down with him on the train. He tells that in the old-time Pullman seats, which swiveled in all directions, they sat face to face for the four-hour trip working on Jacques's English pronunciation of his speech. They were guests at the Dominican House of Studies; after supper with the community they went across Michigan Avenue to the university. The audience, mostly young priests and seminarians, packed the lecture room of McMahon Hall, and Jacques and he looked down on a checkerboard of white, brown, and black, where groups of Dominicans, Franciscans, Carmelites, Paulists, seculars had taken their places. All listened attentively, and it did seem a great success. But in the parlor afterward when my brother asked his impression of the lecture, the rector, Bishop Ryan, said that he had difficulty understanding Jacques.

Jacques had a problem and he knew it. It is a tribute to

his tenacity that he gained in time the remarkable mastery of English that he did. He never ceased to work at it, and the translations of his books were always a source of concern to him. Some of the earlier renderings were very poor, and he constantly sought the help of those who knew French well and understood his thought. I remember the relief he expressed when, in 1959, *The Degrees of Knowledge,* one of his most important books and a key to much of his thinking (written as early as 1932), appeared in a new translation made under the supervision of Dr. Gerald Phelan by doctors of philosophy from the University of Toronto. For years its English-language readers had known it only in a version which, as Jacques said, "was marred by a great many misinterpretations and oversights."

On returning from Toronto in the spring of 1938, Jacques passed through New York, and came to see me at my office. The French Book Club had been sold the year before to Mr. Harry Scherman of the Book-of-the-Month Club, and I had taken a position on the editorial staff of the New York branch of Longmans, Green & Company, a long-established British firm of book publishers. During the fifteen years of my connection with this house, Jacques was to be very helpful in recommending to us books for English translation, and when I was in Paris on scouting expeditions saw to it that I met the authors in person.

His stay in New York that April was very brief. He had been quite ill while in Toronto and looked thin and tired; he did not wish to make many engagements. He found time, however, to go again to the Catholic Worker, where the affectionate interest that awaited him was returned in full measure. This time he answered questions about the use of "pure means," one of the principles which the Catholic Worker was trying to put into practice.

Late in the following summer, Jacques, Raïssa, and Vera sailed on the SS *Florida* to South America, where Jacques had been invited to give a series of lectures in the Argentine. Since 1925 there had been a Jacques Maritain Center at Rio de Janeiro, so on the way to Buenos Aires they stopped in Rio, where Jacques addressed the members of that and other organizations active in social and cultural work. At Buenos Aires he spoke under the auspices of the faculty of arts and letters of the university of that city on "Bergson's Metaphysics" and on "Freudianism and Psychoanalysis" and to the annual Congress of PEN Clubs on "Intelligence and Life."

Both in Buenos Aires and Rio de Janeiro the Maritains had a cordial reception and Jacques's lectures along philosophical lines were well received. The following year, however, there opened in Latin America a campaign of disparagement against him on the part of conservatives when some of his social and political views became known. This was to last for a long time, even though he was always warmly supported by certain socially active elements, especially in Brazil. In the 1940s and 1950s his ideas made a substantial impact on Catholic thinking in Latin America, and by the time of the Second Vatican Council—where many of Maritain's premises prevailed—laymen and churchmen, including prominent members of the hierarchy, had adopted his opinions on social justice and were putting them into vigorous practice. There are many proofs that the Church in Latin America has now become the defender of the poor and underprivileged. It can also be said that the leaders of Christian democratic movements—for instance Eduardo Frei of Chile—have received their inspiration from the writings of Jacques Maritain and from personal contacts with him.

Jacques was again in New York in December 1938 after giving lectures in Toronto, Chicago, and Notre Dame. Raïssa and Vera had started out with him on this trip, but after a visit to Dr. and Mrs. Nef in Chicago, had returned to France. Jacques came alone to give several lectures in and around

New York, and during his stay of some ten days also worked with Harry Binsse, an excellent translator, on several articles that he was writing for American publications. Jacques was much interested in *Liturgical Arts*, a monthly founded for the purpose of improving church architecture and decoration, edited by Harry Binsse and Maurice Lavanoux. While in New York, Jacques was surrounded by a group of young men who, with Binsse and Lavanoux, put themselves at his disposal to aid him in different ways. Among these were members of the staff of *The Commonweal;* Edward Rice and Robert Lax, who were studying at Columbia; Harry McNeill, then teaching at Fordham; and Dan Walsh.

Dan was teaching philosophy at Manhattanville College and lecturing at Columbia on Aquinas and Duns Scotus. It was through him that on this trip Jacques first met Thomas Merton, then studying for his master's degree at Columbia. In his *Seven Storey Mountain,* Thomas Merton wrote: "Dan Walsh had been a student and collaborator of Gilson's and knew Gilson and Maritain well. In fact . . . he introduced me to Maritain at the Catholic Book Club, where this most saintly philosopher had been giving a talk on Catholic Action. I only spoke a few conventional words to Maritain, but the impression you got from this gentle, stooping Frenchman with much gray hair was one of tremendous kindness and simplicity and godliness. And that was enough; you did not need to talk to him. I came away feeling very comforted that there was such a person in the world."

I saw Jacques frequently during this visit to New York, for he came in and out of Longmans for his mail and usually stopped to chat. He was in a relaxed frame of mind, and looking forward to his return to Meudon the day before Christmas. I also saw much of the entourage that surrounded him, and remember the night before he sailed when he came with fifteen of his troop for dinner in my small apartment. Jacques was very fond of young people and at his best among them;

this was a festive occasion. That was the last time I saw him before he, Raïssa, and Vera came to New York during the time of France's disaster in 1940.

Before writing about this, however, I must go back a little to tell something of Jacques's interests and activities in his native country during this period when he was making his early connections in Canada and the United States and was gaining increasing recognition as a figure of importance in American intellectual circles.

VII

A Time of Controversy

France in the 1930s was an ideological battleground. When, in 1933, Jacques Maritain returned from his first visit to America, nothing seemed to have changed on the surface. Behind the scenes, however, the battle lines were forming both on Left and Right for an attack on the institutions of the Third Republic. The attacks were both political and social. On the Left, the Communist Third International was demanding a one-party system and the dictatorship of the proletariat; on the Right, the mounting success of fascism in neighboring countries was arousing hope in the breasts of French reactionaries, whether of monarchist or totalitarian persuasion.

The riots of February 6, 1934, marked the rise in France of the Popular Front in which the Socialist leader, Léon Blum, and the Communist leader, Marcel Cachin, joined hands. On the opposing side, foremost among rightist groups was a movement known as the Croix de Feu, a national organization of fascist tendencies linked to the war veterans. In between was the larger part of the French public, aroused to indignation by the violence shown on both sides and by intrigues in the government revealed by the Stavisky scandal. This case of a big-time swindler with powerful political connections was a blow to parliamentary democracy in general; the governments of France fell in rapid succession. Soon to come were international developments: the Italian invasion of Ethiopia, the Anschluss between Austria and Germany, the Spanish Civil War, the threat from Germany.

Ever since his Action Française experience, Jacques Maritain had pondered on the attitude which he should take in the face of concrete events in political life which raised a moral or spiritual problem. Neither as a philosopher nor as a Christian could he remain indifferent to the crisis just suffered by the people of his country. In the lull that followed the violence of February 6, 1934, he considered that the role of the Christian in the modern world should be defined in a common declaration that would clearly state the principles of Christian humanism. He now concerned himself with the preparation of this statement in collaboration with others of like mind.

The result was the publication in pamphlet form in March 1934 of a manifesto called "*Pour le Bien Commun*" (For the Common Good). Besides Maritain it was signed by fifty-one Catholics prominent in French cultural life. Among these were the philosophers Gabriel Marcel and Étienne Gilson; the writers Stanislas Fumet and Charles du Bos; the artist Jean Hugo; the professors Yves Simon, Jacques Madaule, Olivier Lacombe; the editor Emmanuel Mounier.

Describing the two camps into which France was divided, the manifesto said that "one of them, being especially conscious of present-day political corruption, aspires confusedly to a revolution and an 'order' which in the long run might assume a dictatorial form." The other "is especially aware of present-day social injustice; it aspires more or less to a 'revolution' and an order, but by means of a collective regime oppressive to the human person."

The manifesto went on to say that the Christian could not compromise or "seek a synthesis between two errors." He must apply a moral criterion to such problems as class struggle, capitalism, nationalism, internationalism. These must be viewed "in the light of love and intelligence."

In no way did the signers of the document advocate the creation of a theocracy, nor did they advocate the formation of a Catholic political party, yet they urged Catholics to follow the directives of the Popes in the encyclicals on social justice. Pope Leo XIII had declared that "the greatest scandal of the nineteenth century was that the Church had lost the working classes." In a later encyclical Pope Pius XI had said that capitalists, including certain Catholics, had oppressed the workers "in a spirit of greed," and "taken advantage of religion itself, disguising in its name their true demands."

The manifesto urged Catholics to examine their consciences in these matters, also as to their obedience to the Church concerning peace and patriotism. Patriotic aspirations did not permit feelings of hatred for other countries. Catholics should remind States and nations "of the moral conditions for the organization of an international community which has regard for the rights of the human person and of justice." A national political regime should be neither fascist nor communist; it should represent a moral and spiritual order equally opposed to both. It should oppose totalitarian and collectivist aims as well as the selfish aims of bourgeois individualism. A State should be *pluralist*, "assembling in its organic unity a diversity of groups and of social structures incarnating positive liberties."

Whether or not this manifesto was actually written by Jacques Maritain I never knew, but it was the expression of opinions I heard earlier when I was invited to "sessions on social science" at Meudon. Despite its prudent tone, *"Pour le Bien Commun"* created quite a stir. It was certainly received with sympathy by many of those who were interesting themselves in social problems, whether Catholic, Protestant, or unbelievers. In other quarters it led to criticism of the signers and quite a few attacks on Jacques Maritain personally both from within and without his Church. One began to hear talk of "red Catholics" and even expressions of shocked surprise that in the course of its twenty-eight pages the manifesto asked all Christians to pray for those who had lost their lives in the February riots—whether fascists, communists, or innocent bystanders.

Jacques Maritain thought that the time had come to formulate his own position in such matters both as a philosopher and a Christian. In his *Letter on Independence* (a short book published in 1935), he defined for the first time his views as to what attitude a philosopher *as such* should take in the field of human and political action. He had decided that a philosopher was useful to men only insofar as he remained a philosopher. But to remain a philosopher and act as a philosopher meant to maintain the liberty of philosophy—of all philosophy—in regard to any political party whatsoever. This did not mean that he was personally neutral, but he wished to prepare the metaphysical base for political activity that would be "authentically and vitally Christian." Such activity for temporal aims would not be the same as that of the Catholic Action groups advocated by Pope Pius XI—"for the participation of the laity in the apostolate of the hierarchy"—the purposes of which were in the spiritual order.

In this little book Jacques Maritain says that he found himself in the uncomfortable position of a man who, through a desire for independence, refused to adhere to any of the existing political parties in his country. Because of well-determined concepts, he was *against* each of them: "I am neither to right or left." He then postulates an interesting theory regarding two meanings that can be applied to the terms "right" and "left." Used in the first sense, he says, the words refer to a disposition of temperament, "just as the human being is born bilious or sanguine. All one can do is to correct one's temperament and bring it to an equilibrium where the two tendencies converge. For at the extreme limit of these tendencies a kind of monstrosity unfolds before the mind. . . ." In the second sense of the terms, the political sense, left and right refer to "ideals, energies, and historic formations into which the men of these two opposing temperaments are normally drawn to group themselves."

From the viewpoint of history, Jacques considered that the central problem of the time was "the reintegration of the masses separated from Christianity, principally through the fault of a Christian world unfaithful to its vocation." Since he saw the necessity of new political formations for the temporal political activity of Christians, he set out to formulate a politics which, inspired by the Christian spirit and Christian principles (and which by its justice and humanity would appeal to non-Christians as well), would engage only the responsibility of the citizens who conduct it, without being dictated by or involving the Church. The Christian, he wrote, should be in every corner, and everywhere remain free to work in the temporal structure of society for the dignity of the human person, for the common good, and for moral and spiritual values.

In seeking to carry out the program he had indicated, Jacques Maritain soon became involved in a number of debates as national and international issues presented themselves. It was through *Esprit* and its editor Emmanuel Mounier that he entered the lists. The brawny young man with the looks of an "overgrown schoolboy" was indefatigable in bringing to the fore issues in the political, social, and philosophical area which he thought should not only be debated but acted upon by *Esprit* and its followers. There is no doubt that Jacques approved the over-all objectives Mounier had outlined to him, and wished to aid in an effort he considered laudable and in accord with his convictions. Even though he saw no objection to *Esprit*'s running articles by contributors of divergent views, he was particularly anxious that there be no departure from sound philosophical and doctrinal bases in the positions taken by the review itself. He therefore agreed to work closely with Mounier and give his opinion on articles to be published.

Although twenty-five years of age separated them, Jacques Maritain and Emmanuel Mounier were linked by a deep and abiding personal friendship. Their collaboration, however, was not as peaceful as has been generally assumed. The correspondence between the two[1] shows that, even if together on fundamental choices, Jacques did not agree with various forms of political activity proposed by Mounier. If in certain cases Jacques was able to rectify or moderate statements in the

---

[1] See *Jacques Maritain–Emmanuel Mounier, 1929–1939*, ed. by Jacques Petit (Paris: Desclée de Brouwer, 1973).

articles submitted to him, he did not see them all in advance. Under the pressure of getting out a monthly review—or perhaps because he thought that Jacques would have reservations —Mounier did not show everything to him. And it is true that at the beginning of their collaboration, Mounier had stressed *Esprit*'s editorial independence. However, when he got into trouble with the ecclesiastical authorities, which he often did, it was always to Jacques that he turned to smooth out the difficulties. This was not always easy, as when, in 1935, there was a real possibility that *Esprit* might be condemned by Rome along with other "left-wing Catholic" publications. It was largely due to Jacques Maritain and his influence with important members of the hierarchy that this did not happen.

Some of *Esprit*'s difficulties stemmed from the way Mounier handled the matter of conscientious objection to military service. In a column headed "Catholics and National Defense" he protested a warlike article by General de Castelnau which had appeared in a Paris daily. General de Castelnau was the president of a large organization called the National Catholic Federation which had great influence in conservative Catholic circles. He had lost three sons in the First World War and was outraged when in the course of his published protest Mounier demanded: "General, aren't three sons enough?" Even had Jacques approved the position of the conscientious objector, which is dubious from his correspondence with Mounier,[2] he would have avoided such acrimony. Ironically,

---

[2] Judging from a letter written to Mounier in June 1935, Jacques Maritain at that time regarded conscientious objection as "an illusion calculated to mislead generous spirits," but deplored the harshness of the legal measures invoked against them. In fact, he later signed a petition protesting these measures, but with reservations on the part of some of the signers as to their personal position on conscientious objection per se. Although Maritain regarded war as a great evil and respected those whose conscience forbade them to engage in violence of any kind, he believed that a war could be just under very limited conditions as in the case of legitimate defense when a country has been unjustly attacked. But "the most terrible anguish for a Christian is precisely this of knowing that there can be justice in the use of horrible means." See English edition of *True Humanism* (New York: Charles Scribner's Sons, 1938), pp. 241–42.

he was the chief sufferer from such polemics, and General de Castelnau—also doubtless because of his own strong convictions—joined forces with other conservative elements in denouncing more than one project with which Jacques Maritain was associated.

Jacques did not retreat before these attacks, but met with calm both flattery and insults. He considered that he should clarify still further his role as a speculative thinker on temporal matters. This he set out to do in a major work that he spent much time and thought in preparing for publication. *True Humanism*, published in 1936, was the expansion and revision of six lectures on "The Spiritual and Temporal Problems of a New Christendom" which he had delivered two years earlier at the summer school of the University of Santander, Spain.

The philosophy called "practical" by Aristotle and Aquinas, he wrote, is still philosophy but "unlike metaphysics or natural philosophy is from the outset directed to action as its object." In dealing with the complex structures of modern society, he did not claim to speak with the authority of Saint Thomas; he wished nevertheless to tap the mainspring of the Thomistic spirit and doctrine to trace the historical development of Western humanism, to defend what remained in it of Christian values, and to propose some solutions. In the course of his work he pointed out the deviation from "true humanism" of philosophies having only materialistic ends in view. This led to the discussion of such errors as communism, fascism and its derivatives, as well as the remnants under various forms of the exaggerated individualism of the nineteenth century.

The "new Christendom" outlined in *True Humanism* is presented not as a repetition of that of the Middle Ages but "as conceivable today" even in a world where Maritain recognized the conditions as far from ideal. The coexistence of believers and unbelievers in the temporal city is placed in a society marked by civil toleration, an economy freed from the capitalist yoke, recognition of the rights of the human personality, and in a "personalist democracy" based on the achievement of a fraternal community.

True Humanism was regarded by Jacques's followers as a veritable charter for social action. His warning against political combinations with parties based on extreme ideologies was soon to serve them in good stead. In 1936, the Popular Front was installed in power with Léon Blum at the head of a coalition government of socialists and communists. During the electoral campaign the communist leader Maurice Thorez proclaimed: "We stretch out our hand to you Catholics, workers, artisans, peasants, because you are our brothers and live under the weight of the same hardships as we." Catholics were urged to form with communists "a common front against fascism." The anti-religious propaganda of French communists was ordered suspended as the Communist Party sought recruits among the Christian syndicates, Catholic youth groups, and other members of the Catholic social movement. With the exception of a few free lances, the outstretched hand was not and could not be accepted by Catholics, especially after the clear condemnation of "atheistic communism" in the papal encyclical *Divini Redemptoris* of March 1937. During this period the Dominicans of *Sept* and the editors of *Esprit* adopted an unequivocal stand against the Trojan-horse policy of the communist political leaders, just as a year earlier they had protested the fascist Italian adventure in Ethiopia when it was represented by certain rightist French Catholics as "in defense of the Occident."

We now come to one of the most controversial episodes in Jacques's career. It was on the basis of the ideologies involved that he took the stand he did on the Spanish Civil War. In Spain any theoretical discussion had passed to the plane of war with the victory in the elections of 1936 of the *Frente Popular*, composed of the working masses, socialists, communists, and syndicalists, who soon were quarreling among themselves. This state of disorder was met by a military uprising against the new government led by General Francisco Franco with the support of army officers, part of the police, civil servants, the clergy, landowners, and industrialists; these forces soon received the military aid of Germany and Italy. The opposing Loyalist side was supported by the Popular Front Party, the separatists in Catalonia and the Basque Provinces (many of whom were Catholic), the International Brigades formed abroad, and military aid from the U.S.S.R.

Germans and Italians on one side and Russians on the other tried out in Spain the newest makes of weapons, planes, and tanks. Loyalist mobs in an atmosphere of anarchy began a ruthless persecution of the Catholic Church and its clergy. According to the most conservative estimates, 160 churches and convents were destroyed by fire, ten bishops were killed, some thousands of priests and men and women members of religious orders were hunted down, tortured, and put to death. On the other side, Franco brought in Moors, Germans, and Italians to combat the Spanish people; his forces bombed open cities and towns, with resulting destruction of life, property, and works of art.

In France opinions were divided on the subject of the Spanish conflict. It should be said that in the Blum government there was a strong element of sympathy for the Loyalists, and with its more or less open consent International Brigades were formed on French soil. At least a hundred French planes were purchased on the initiative of individuals and sent to the aid of the Loyalists in the first year of the struggle. However, the French government—locked in a class struggle at home, with the flight of capital, strikes, occupation of factories—proposed with England a nonintervention agreement, and other governments joined in this with varying degrees of sincerity.

The position of the Catholic Church toward the ideologies underlying the various totalitarian forms of government involved had been stated by Pope Pius XI in March 1937 in three encycylicals succeeding one another in quick succession. The first, *Mit brennender Sorge*, was in defense of persecuted Catholicism in Germany and a condemnation of the Nazi and racial theories of National Socialism. (As early as 1931, the Pope had denounced fascism in Italy.) The second encyclical was *Divini Redemptoris*, condemning the persecution of the Church by atheistic communism in Russia, Spain, and Mexico, and also urging a reconstruction of the labor world on Christian and humane foundations. The third encyclical, *Nos es muy*, dealt with the de-Christianization of life in Mexico, on the rights of Catholics as citizens, on the character and limits of resistance to constituted powers.

Because Jacques Maritain thought it was impossible to sustain the thesis that there was nothing but evil (communism) on one side and on the other nothing but good (Catholicism and patriotism), he rejected the idea of a "holy war" proclaimed by Franco's supporters. The only thing he ever wrote on the subject was a preface to Alfredo Mendizábel's book *The Martyrdom of Spain*. "Not to side with Salamanca," he said there, "does not mean siding with Valencia. . . . It is a horrible sacrilege to murder priests, even if they are fascists. . . . And it is another sacrilege, and also a horrible one, to murder the poor in the name of religion, even if they are Marxists. . . ." The tragedy, he said, was that "for centuries in Spain, religion had been confused with clerical power, and the external show of spiritual authority had become the chief thing in religious matters; the clergy, to find support among the privileged classes, appeared too often as the pastors of these rather than of the masses."

In February 1937, Maritain signed with other prominent Frenchmen a protest against the bombing of Madrid by the Franco forces, and in May that same year he and his friends publicly protested the strafing by German planes of Guernica, a small Basque market town, where women and children were killed by bombs. This did not mean, he said, that he condoned the murder of thousands of ecclesiastics and Catholic laymen on the grounds of their religion.

Because members of the Catholic Church were engaged on both sides, Jacques began his endeavor to promote "civil peace" between Spanish Catholics. He was instrumental in forming and presided the French Committee for Civil and Religious Peace in Spain. Among its members were Louis Gillet of the French Academy, Louis le Fur and Georges Scelles, professors of international law at the Sorbonne, Bishop E. Beaupin, and François Mauriac. This committee made contact with Catholic members of the Loyalist government and the Catholic Basque leaders in an effort to abate religious persecution by their partisans; the committee also undertook relief work among the Spanish refugees who crossed into France as the war drew to an end, an effort sponsored by Cardinal Verdier, archbishop of Paris.

Jacques Maritain's stand on the Spanish Civil War was misunderstood by the French public on both sides (not to mention many people in America). Even some of his friends turned against him. There was a break with Paul Claudel. Other influential Catholic writers, among them François Mauriac and Georges Bernanos, took the same attitude as Jacques, as did his close collaborators and new friends among Spanish political exiles. Among the visitors to Meudon there were now prominent Spanish and Basque personalities, devout Catholics, caught on the horns of the dilemma between fascism and communism.

During the whole period of the Spanish Civil War the debate continued to rage in the press between conservatives and those expressing sympathy with leftist causes. Jacques kept an eye on *Esprit*, anxious that there be no departure from sound doctrinal positions. At his suggestion, Mounier often checked with the theologian Abbé Journet of the University of Fribourg on such matters as the limits of possible collaboration between Christians and unbelievers. General de

Castelnau was on the alert for any slip, and Henri Massis attacked Mounier bitterly in a much discussed book on Maurras, still defending the views of the Action Française leader. There was a campaign in the daily *Écho de Paris* against a certain number of organs, denounced as a press monopoly of "Marxist Christians," which named five Catholic publications including *Esprit*. There was a new threat of condemnation by Rome when representatives of the French Catholic Action organizations and press were convoked to the Vatican in May 1936. Jacques Maritain spent many hours advising Mounier on how to present his case and in personal approaches to the hierarchy on behalf of his friend's review. Through the intervention of important French ecclesiastics, including Cardinal Verdier, *Esprit*'s condemnation was avoided.

Another publication in which Jacques was interested was not so lucky. The liberal weekly *Sept*, under the editorship of Father Bernadot of the Latour Maubourg community, was suppressed in 1938 by order of Father Gillet, General of the Dominicans. In an interview with the ambassador of France to the Vatican, François Charles-Roux, Father Gillet explained that this was not a "doctrinal condemnation" but "a measure of internal discipline" in his order because of dissensions among the Dominicans of various countries raised by the attitude *Sept* had taken regarding political and international events and especially the Spanish Civil War. In agreement with Pope Pius XI personally, he had agreed that the suppression of *Sept* was "in the interests of the Church."

The disaster to his friends at Le Cerf was a blow to Jacques Maritain. It confirmed him, however, in his belief that political matters had best be left to the Christian laity. Only a short time later, in 1938, he took part in the founding of *Temps Présent*, a paper along the lines of *Sept* but more prudent in tone. Staffed by laymen under the editorship of Stanislas Fumet, a man of great good will and equanimity, it tried to bring a new Christian spirit into homes, neighborhoods, and professions, and to suggest definite and particular means for promoting cultural and spiritual understanding among the different classes of society. For instance, bureaucrats were urged to pay less attention to red tape, and to consider human needs; teachers were reminded to think less of their careers and more of their responsibility as educators of the young; employers, of consideration for their employees; capitalists, of the welfare of their workers; priests, of their duty to teach the papal encyclicals. Articles along these and general cultural lines were contributed to the paper by Jacques Maritain, François Mauriac, and other now famous writers.

Tempo Présent steered clear of trouble with the ecclesiastical and any other authorities until the armistice of 1940 when it was suppressed by Vichy "because of its general tendencies." Publication of *Esprit* was also halted at this time. However, after a prolonged interruption, when many Catholic organs were transferred to the Unoccupied Zone along with other newspapers and reviews, Stanislas Fumet was permitted to resume publication of *Temps Présent* under another name, *Temps Nouveau*. Mounier had been mobilized at the beginning of the war into the auxiliary of an Alpine regiment, and in the environs of Grenoble carried on *Esprit* in a reduced form and in continual struggle with Vichy censorship. Both *Esprit* and *Temps Nouveau* and the movements they represented were to become centers of resistance to the Germans made by French Catholics.

During those years of controversy in the 1930s, torn on one hand by the worldwide depression and on the other by ideological controversies that led to war, the life of the household at Meudon went on as before. Julien Green, an occasional visitor who came to discuss with Jacques his literary and personal perplexities, could write of "the marvelous peace that reigned in that house on the rue du Parc." Outside the gatherings on Sunday afternoons and the reception of callers

—carefully orchestrated by Vera—Jacques, when not away teaching or lecturing, worked in philosophical calm. The family prayed together in their small chapel, and Raïssa still spent many hours alone in prayer and meditation.

Besides his books on political and social philosophy, Jacques saw published in those years his *Philosophy of Nature* and *Science and Wisdom*, and a number of shorter essays and articles on metaphysical subjects. He continued to edit the series of books at Desclée de Brouwer, supplied prefaces to the works of other writers, and wrote a text to accompany the publication in book form of Marc Chagall's biblical illustrations. Together he and Raïssa worked on a new and enlarged edition of *Art and Scholasticism*, and on two new books on art, *The Frontiers of Poetry* and *The Situation of Poetry* (1938).

Raïssa always said that she was by instinct "apprehensive" about anything in the way of political activity; in that domain she saw what Saint Paul calls the evil of the times. Although she loyally supported Jacques in his endeavor to draw up a blueprint for a better world, subjects in the realm of spirituality and art were more congenial to her. In those years she was doing quite a bit of writing of her own: in her *Journal*, in letters to friends, including priests, who consulted her about their spiritual problems, several translations from Latin into French of little-known writings of Thomas Aquinas and his commentator John of Saint Thomas. For children, she wrote her *Angel of the Schools*, a simple and touching life of Saint Thomas, illustrated by Gino Severini; this I translated into English for publication by Sheed & Ward the following year. Raïssa wrote poems which she said were only for herself, but in 1935 Vera and Jacques persuaded her to publish a selection. *La Vie Donnée* (The Offered Life) was so praised that the printing was quickly exhausted; in 1939 she added those poems to others that appeared under the title *Lettre de Nuit* (Night

Letter). The first collection was almost entirely on spiritual subjects; the second, reflections of human experience—on love, friendship, suffering, the beauties of nature, and sometimes on the impact of a great work of art.[3]

Raïssa knew a great deal about music, and she kept in close touch with the work of the musicians among her friends. She and Jacques were particularly devoted to the Russian-born composer Arthur Lourié and his wife Ella, and Raïssa made many efforts to further the career of a man she regarded as one of the important musical geniuses of the time. To get his *Concerto Spirituale* produced she formed a choral society with the aid of Roland Manuel. Among its sponsors were Alfred Cortot, Serge Koussevitzky, Maurice Brilliant, Louis Laloy, Marc Chagall, besides many other writers, musicians, and critics; François Mauriac presided this committee. The first public audition of Lourié's *Concerto* took place in 1936 in the Paris auditorum of the Salle Pleyel, under the direction of Charles Munch, and with the participation of two choirs. Few prominent members of the French musical world failed to attend, and the director of the BBC orchestra came from London for the occasion. Raïssa was delighted when, as she and Jacques sat in the Louriés' box, they saw Arturo Toscanini walk in and take his seat in the audience.

Raïssa and Vera still carried on the preparatory work for the annual spiritual retreats of the Thomist Center held at Meudon. In the fall of 1937 nearly three hundred persons arrived for the three-day session, and Jacques later told of the deep devotion and fraternal atmosphere that marked this assembly in spite of the divergent opinions of the participants on national and international affairs. He recalled this Meudon experience later when, in New York in 1941, he suggested a similar retreat for the numerous French citizens of varying

---

[3] After Raïssa's death, thirty of her poems were translated into English by a Benedictine of Stanbrook and appeared under the title *Patriarch Tree* (Worcester: Stanbrook Abbey Press, 1965).

political views who arrived in the United States at the time of the fall of France.[4]

In February 1938, Jacques gave a public lecture in Paris in the prestigious series *"Les Ambassadeurs"* at the Marigny Theater. The subject was anti-Semitism. The persecution of Jews in Germany and Austria had brought many refugees into France, and they had been received for the most part with sympathy; any anti-Jewish legislation at that time seemed impossible, yet certain racist articles had appeared in the press. Jacques was eager to remind his compatriots, and especially Catholics, of what their attitude should be toward what Saint Paul calls "the mystery of Israel."

His approach to the problem was religious, historical, and metaphysical, and depicted anti-Semitism as inadmissible for members of the Christian religion, descended from Judaism, and as historically and scientifically unsound. His temperate analysis was well received by most, yet there were criticisms from certain Catholics who saw it as an "exclusively supernaturalist interpretation of the problem," which ignored its economic and cultural aspects, and was unsupported by the teachings of the Church. Six months later, in September 1938, Pope Pius XI made his famous public statement: "Anti-Semitism is a movement in which we Christians can take no part whatever. . . . Anti-Semitism is unacceptable. Spiritually, we are Semites."

During this same September, at the time of the German take-over of Czechoslovakia, there was grave danger of war and the French army was mobilized. Many of the Maritain friends, including priests, were called into the service. The Thomist retreat could not be held that fall, but there were "days of recollection" for members of the Thomist Center, some smaller gatherings, and meetings with Mounier and

---

[4] The retreat was in fact held in New York at the Convent of the Helpers of the Holy Souls under the direction of Father John LaFarge, S.J., and the Dominicans, Father Couturier and Father Ducatillon.

others anxious to have Jacques's advice on what attitude they should take in the crisis. (At that time Mounier was inclined to pacifist views and was quite annoyed when their friend Georges Bidault wrote for *L'Aube*, a liberal paper, an article which Mounier considered as fomenting war.)

The Maritains were in a quandary themselves, for Jacques had lecture engagements in the United States and planned on taking Raïssa and Vera along. Not knowing whether they would be able to leave, they packed and unpacked their luggage, made and unmade arrangements for a possible absence of several months. However, the Munich Pact was signed on September 30, and they left France early in October, though not at all assured that "peace for our time" had been achieved by the agreement made with Hitler by the French, English, and Italian statesmen.

After their safe return from the American trip, the Maritains spent Christmas at home in Meudon. Jacques resumed his teaching at the Institut Catholique, his editorial work, writing, and lecturing. On February 8, 1939, he gave for the second and last time a remarkable public address at the Marigny Theater (in the same *"Ambassadeur"* series), which was remembered with emotion by all who heard it. Rereading the copy which he sent me, I can but agree with Stanislas Fumet that "there is not a fissure in this noble edifice." The pessimism of the title which Jacques chose, "The Twilight of Civilization," is but relative, but after describing in thoughtful terms the false philosophies that had brought Western civilization to its present pass, he reiterated his faith in the new humanism on which he had long pondered, one based on Christian principles of justice and brotherly love. It is touching to note that at this time he put much hope in American democracy as a system in which Christian values were vitally integrated.

That year Jacques published his *Quatre Essais sur l'Esprit dans Sa Condition Charnelle*, a work on psychology. In it he developed within the Thomist framework such themes as Freudianism and psychoanalysis, signs and symbols, and natural mystical experience. In May, he delivered a lecture at Oxford University on "The Human Person and Society," and wrote a number of articles.

Jacques and Raïssa spent the summer of 1939 near the Benedictine abbeys of Solesmes and Fontgombault, and were at the latter when the Second World War began on September 3, 1939. Raïssa's writings are filled with dark forebodings at this time. Although I am not certain, it is possible that Jacques, like many Frenchmen, had hopes at first of a French victory, even though he realized that it would be won at great cost. At any rate, he wrote during this time articles for the French and American press with such titles as "Europe Will Not Perish!" "The Necessary Renewal," and "On Just War."

This was the period of the *"Sitzkrieg,"* the calm before the storm. At the end of the year, Jacques prepared to leave France for a lengthy lecture tour, having been urged by the Ministry of Cultural Relations to carry out his usual schedule in Canada and the United States. On January 4, 1940, he sailed from Marseilles with Raïssa and Vera. He could not have known that five long years would pass before he would again set foot on the soil of France.

New York, 1940–45

Following the French defeat, Jacques, Raïssa, and Vera spent the hot, stifling summer at the old Brevoort Hotel on lower Fifth Avenue in New York. I saw them often during those anxious days; my office was close by and I was not without my own worries. The United States was not yet at war with Germany, and my brother Tom, since 1937 manager of the French edition of *Vogue* and representative of the Condé Nast group in Europe, had remained in occupied Paris to close down in orderly fashion the publishing interests of the firm. He was completely cut off from the outer world and I was most uneasy about his situation until he returned to the United States seven months later.

American newspapers and radio had carried in full and often contradictory detail the shattering news of the German entry into Paris, the armistice, the enemy occupation of two thirds of the country, the dissolution of the Third Republic, and the installation of the Vichy government. Soon there were arrivals of those of the Maritains' friends who had been able to flee France in the last hours before the occupants sealed the frontiers. Many came with sad stories of their personal adventures, of the crumbling of civic life, and of the witch-hunts conducted by the Germans in occupied territory. Jacques was to learn that very soon after the German entry into Paris, the Gestapo had gone looking for him at the Institut Catholique, as one of the known leaders of anti-fascist ideology.

Realizing that a return home was impossible, Jacques had little choice except to remain in New York. He now dedicated much effort to the help of his exiled compatriots. For as the military rout of France became inevitable, it was obvious that things would go hard for persons known for their liberal views, and especially for those of Jewish extraction. In most immediate danger were the refugees from Germany or other totalitarian regimes who had earlier settled in France. Many of Jacques's friends, stranded in Spain, in Portugal, or in the precarious haven of North Africa, managed to get in touch with him for aid.

The entrance visa to the United States was the crux of the problem, calling for activity and sponsorship by someone already on American shores. Jacques often turned for help to Dr. Alvin Johnson, president of the New School for Social Research in New York. Even before the war, Dr. Johnson had been indefatigable in his efforts to find posts in various fields for teachers who had left their homelands as the cloud of Nazism closed over central Europe. For some he had found positions at the New School. These were Germans, Austrians, Czechs; there were also Italians. Now it was the turn of the French. In the autumn of 1940 and the winter of 1940–41, it was he who aided Jacques to secure entry permits. And later on, the university-in-exile known as the École Libre des Hautes Études gathered French and Belgian scholars under the New School's hospitable roof. Of the École Libre I shall say more a bit further on, as Jacques was to be actively connected with it.

Early that summer he began the writing of a short book to analyze for the American public the sociopolitical and military causes which had brought unfortunate France to her knees. In it, he wished particularly to express his inexhaustible faith in the French people, whose failings, he insisted, had been *political* but not *moral*. Although he worked on this book almost every day, he did not finish *A Travers le Désastre* (English title, *France My Country*), until the following November, because kaleidoscopic events made it difficult to form an opinion. On June 18, he had listened with emotion to General de Gaulle's famous broadcast from London, opposing the armistice and appealing for resistance; later he was encouraged by the news that several French colonies in Africa had rallied to the general's movement and that he had set up a Council for the Defense of the French Empire, which became in September 1941 the National Committee for Free France. Even so, de Gaulle's future intentions were unclear, and much as Jacques admired his courage, at the time he wrote his book he did not express unqualified adherence to de Gaulle's movement.

At the same time Jacques followed with growing dismay the record of Vichy as it sought to maintain the semblance of a government under the heel of the enemy. He did not denounce Pétain personally, but Jacques noted that, despite the aged marshal's efforts to improve the lot of France and of French prisoners of war and to "collaborate honorably" with the Germans, Pétain had been forced little by little to yield to harsh demands. Clearly, Jacques thought, no hope could be placed in a regime that was not free in its decisions and which included many reactionary forces. His book was, in fact, an appeal to his countrymen who remained in France to cling to its ideals and cleanse its politics and social inequities.

As Jacques wanted to have this book appear as quickly as possible, he made advance arrangements for its publication. In New York a new firm, Éditions de la Maison Française, had recently been started, to issue in their own language the work of numerous French writers who had come to the United States, among them André Maurois, Jules Romains, Julien Green, Antoine de Saint-Exupéry. This firm had agreed to accept *A Travers le Désastre* as soon as it was ready, and brought it out early in 1941. It was secretly introduced into France, mimeographed at a press at Gap, then reprinted by Éditions de Minuit, an underground publishing firm in the Unoccupied Zone. Jacques learned that it was widely circulated among the resistance groups now forming in that territory, and that he was often quoted in *Cahiers du Témoignage Chrétien*, the most influential of the clandestine periodicals which sprang up at that time. We will also remember that Stanislas Fumet and Emmanuel Mounier had gone to southern France and were making every effort to continue the publications they edited: *Temps Présent* and *Esprit*. These periodicals and their editors had many followers and, although not entirely free to express their thoughts in print, became focal points for resistance to Vichy "realism" by Catholics and others who shared their views.[1]

For the publication of his book in English, Jacques came to Longmans, Green with an attractive proposition. It was to start with our firm a series to be called "Golden Measure Books," similar to the ones he had edited for Plon and Desclée de Brouwer in Paris; he and I would be co-editors of this series. The first volume to appear would be his little book on France, and he suggested works in progress by other writers. The Longmans management acquiesced in the arrangements he proposed, and I embarked on a happy collaboration with him, moving as quickly as possible to get his book translated and to the printer. The English version, *France My Country*, also appeared early in 1941.

In the meantime, Raïssa had been working since the previous summer on a book of memoirs, first suggested to her by Dr. Étienne Gilson when she and Vera had been in Toronto with Jacques. She was suffering intensely from the debacle, both for herself and for others, but the writing of this book about her childhood in Russia, her romance with Jacques, their early life and work together, the precious friendships of those days, the road she and Jacques had followed into the Catholic Church was in many ways an outlet and a comfort to her. When, at the end of a year, she had finished the first volume

[1] See Jacques Duquesne, *Les Catholiques Français sous l'Occupation* (Paris: Grasset, 1966).

of *Les Grandes Amitiés*, she asked if I would myself translate it into English. This work I gladly undertook outside office hours, deeply interested in the insight it gave into the characters and early experiences of two remarkable people about whose private lives very little was then known. Raïssa's earlier published writings, except for her poetry, and all of Jacques's books had been written on a philosophical level and in more or less technical terms. These memoirs, intended for the general public, describe simply and with touching details the salient events of the Maritains' lives up through the First World War.

As I translated her book, I came often to Raïssa to clear up certain points and ask for further information. As our association and friendship deepened, I appreciated even more her gentleness and simplicity, the charity of her judgments, the remarkable range of her mind, her modest estimate of herself. She gave me details she had not put into her book, showed me photographs, and gave me books and papers on which I have drawn for the present writing.

The first volume of Raïssa's memoirs was published in French by the Éditions de la Maison Française (in 1942) and at the same time in the "Golden Measure" series at Longmans under the title *We Have Been Friends Together*. The many heart-warming letters she received from its readers encouraged Raïssa to embark on the writing of a second volume.

In September of 1940, the Maritains had moved from the hotel to a furnished apartment at 30 Fifth Avenue. There they were to remain until the end of the war, "setting up," as one of their friends said, "a veritable island of French territory in the heart of New York City." Jacques believed that it was important for them to maintain at all times an atmosphere of firm hope in the presence of their fellow Frenchmen, and many were those who came to them for advice and encouragement in those difficult days. The Maritains' hospitality, however, was not confined to their compatriots and they soon were also welcoming into their home a new circle of American friends.

Brave as was the front they presented to the world, this adjustment to a new life was very trying for the Maritains, who felt themselves uprooted in surroundings and circumstances so different from those of their previous lives. Cut off from any financial resources he had in France, Jacques had to plunge into a heavy schedule of lecturing and the writing of books and articles. In 1941, he began to give courses at Princeton and Columbia universities, filled his engagements in Canada and the Middle West, and published with Scribner two books—*Ransoming the Time* and *The Person and the Common Good*—and with Longmans *The Living Thoughts of Saint Paul*. The first English translations of Jacques's books were issued by the publishing house of Sheed & Ward, which did pioneer work in making known to readers in Great Britain and the United States the works of a number of continental Catholic thinkers. But before coming to America, he had contracted for the English edition of certain future works to be issued jointly by Geoffrey Bles in London and by Scribner in New York; as these were readied, Jacques worked with the courteous Scribner editor William Savage. Another editor and friend was Dr. Ruth Nanda Anshen, at whose request Jacques contributed a chapter to *Freedom: Its Meaning*, a collection of outstanding opinions prepared by her for the firm of Harcourt, Brace. At her request, Jacques also later wrote chapters for inclusion in her "World Perspectives" series published by Harper.

At this time as Jacques was submerged in work, Raïssa was particularly unhappy, distressed by the news that seeped through to her from France, missing the peace and quiet of Meudon. She shrank from the bustle and noise of the big city around her and spent much time at her desk, leaving the apartment as rarely as possible. Even so, she graciously received visitors, and coped as best she could with the domestic problems that arose.

It was in this department of practical affairs that Vera, as always, excelled. The outside world held no terrors for her, and she could be seen frequently on Sixth Avenue darting into shops and chain stores as she made her wishes known to tradesmen in limited but voluble English. Raïssa had a wider knowledge of that language and read and understood it quite well, but would almost never speak it, fearing to make mistakes. Vera, on the other hand, had no such qualms as she answered the telephone and struggled with domestic help and repairmen, letting the verbal chips fall where they might. And at this time she excelled in another way: Jacques and Raïssa both told that when they were alone, and inclined to give way to pessimism and quasi-despair over the outcome of the war, Vera always assured them of her conviction that France would be saved. Somehow she managed to restore their spirits, even though she, in turn, later confessed that for three years she had been inwardly torn by uncertainty and desolation.

After Pearl Harbor in December 1941, when the United States entered the war on the side of the Allies, Jacques broadcast frequently to France under the auspices of the Office of War Information. He also played an active role in the foundation of the École Libre des Hautes Études, housed at the New School for Social Research, which opened its doors in February 1942. Dr. Alvin Johnson had thought at first to integrate the French and Belgian refugee scholars into his existing faculty of graduate studies, but a new plan had been developed. Professor Gustave Cohen, professor of medieval literature at the Sorbonne, and one of the first arrivals, proposed the setting up of a university-in-exile, using French as the medium of instruction and issuing certificates that would fulfill the requirements for civil service positions in the African areas controlled by General de Gaulle. He got in touch with de Gaulle and received his warm approval of an institution which would be at that time "the only Free French university in existence." To its founders the general sent a modest grant from his treasury, and Henri Bonnet, the unofficial ambassador of Free France in the United States, gave them much help.

While this project was being set up, Jacques had worked closely with Dr. Johnson, with Professor Cohen, and with the art historian Henri Focillon, who became the École's first president. Other renowned scholars with whom Jacques was associated at this time were the mathematician Jacques Hadamard; the historian of science Alexander Koyré; the international law professor Boris Mirkine-Guetzevitch; the Belgian professor Henri Grégoire. When Professor Focillon died in 1943, Jacques became the second president of the École Libre. All along it had received unstinting cooperation from French professors in other American universities and from their American colleagues, and Jacques sought to further these relationships. Among other exchanges, his friend Dr. John Nef came from Chicago to lecture at the École Libre, and Jacques sent a delegation from his faculty to visit Dr. Nef's Committee of Social Thought at the University of Chicago.

In late 1942, General de Gaulle invited Jacques Maritain and the diplomat-poet Alexis Saint-Léger Léger (Saint-John Perse) to enter his National Committee of Free France. In respectful terms both refused, for the political situation had become most complex. After the American landing in Algiers in November of that year, General de Gaulle had joined his Free French forces to the American and British armies in North Africa. However, following the assassination of Admiral Darlan, who had brought them over to the Allies, the regular French forces there had passed under the leadership of General Giraud. Especially in American eyes, Giraud was regarded at that time as the guardian of French interests, whereas the British had made commitments to General de Gaulle. In any case, as the year 1942 drew to its close, Jacques had taken on so many obligations that he did not feel he could leave the United States, nor did he think of himself in any other role than that of a philosopher and teacher.

During this same year, one of the Maritains' tragic concerns was the fate of their Jewish friends who had been unable to leave France. Even when they reached unoccupied territory, anti-Semitic decrees gradually imposed by the Vichy government under German pressure led to the handing over to the Gestapo of a number of persons the Maritains had known intimately. Among them were French citizens, the veterans of two wars. The fact that some of those of Jewish descent had long been Christians did not save them. News of such things was slow to reach New York, but as time passed the Maritains heard of the deportation to Germany of Babet Jacob, a godchild of Raïssa's, together with her eighty-year-old mother and a younger brother, Manuel, of whom Jacques was particularly fond. (It was only at the end of the war that they learned that Babet and her mother had been thrown into the gas chamber at Buchenwald, the brother shot down.) The elder brother of Jean and Suzanne Marx, who were among the Maritains' oldest friends and frequent visitors to Meudon, was also killed. There were other victims, including the poet-artist Max Jacob, who had for many years lived in retirement at the Benedictine abbey of Saint-Benoît-sur-Loire; in February 1944 he was seized in the cloister, and died of pneumonia in the prison camp of Drancy.

Anguished by these events, Jacques spoke out and championed the Jews as he had always done. Already one of the chapters of his book *Ransoming the Time*, published in 1941, had included a philosophical consideration of anti-Semitism. Entitled "The Mystery of Israel," it was an updating of the views he had expressed in his prewar lecture at the Marigny Theater in Paris and in his historical study *A Christian Looks at the Jewish Question*, issued in 1939 by Longmans, Green. Now he continued to write articles against racism for various

American publications. All this won for him the appreciation of the Jewish community. Dr. Louis Finkelstein, president of the Jewish Theological Seminary, invited him to speak on several occasions at the institution he headed. Jacques also took an active interest in the National Conference of Christians and Jews, presided by Dr. Carlton J. H. Hayes of Columbia University. In early 1943 Jacques chaired at the École Libre the annual meeting of the Institute of Comparative Law, where reports were made on the genesis of racist laws in Germany, their extension over Europe, and the wartime application of anti-Semitic decrees in France.

Jacques's views on these subjects were vigorously supported by *The Commonweal,* to which he was a frequent contributor; he was often in consultation with outstanding Catholics in New York, both laymen and clergy. Among his close friends were George Shuster, the president of Hunter College, and Father John LaFarge, a Jesuit, influential in social and cultural movements.

One of the Maritains' friends at Meudon and Clamart, Helen Iswolsky, had arrived in the United States after spending a year in Unoccupied France. She brought with her an aged mother, and for the second time the two ladies of distinguished Russian background had to begin life afresh in a foreign country. Helen had earlier written several important books on Soviet Russia, and was recognized in Paris as an able journalist whose work was in demand; this career she had to leave behind when she fled from Paris to Unoccupied France, where she awaited the opportunity to cross the Spanish border, reach Lisbon, and from there the United States. On arriving in New York, she got in touch with the Maritains, and I saw her often at their apartment.

Helen Iswolsky was an Orthodox Russian who had become a Roman Catholic of the Eastern rite, and had long done what she could to encourage the dialogue between Orthodox and Roman Catholics. Jacques encouraged her to write a book about this and about other ecumenical and social movements with which she had been associated in France during the ten years preceding the war. As we know, she had already been identified with the work of Nicolas Berdiaeff. She had also collaborated with the Dominican Fathers of Le Cerf, with Mounier and the personalist movement of the *Esprit* group, with Stanislas Fumet and *Temps Présent*. The American public knew very little at that time about the struggle that had gone on in France for social and spiritual regeneration, and in Unoccupied France, Helen had seen signs that it had not been abandoned. Jacques wanted her to say what could be safely published about this at the time, and wrote the preface to Helen's book *Light Before Dusk*. I edited it, and saw it published by Longmans in the "Golden Measure" series.

Soon thereafter Helen began her work with the Office of War Information, broadcasting a program addressed to the women of France. Another of the Maritains' friends then working with the Office of War Information was the novelist Julien Green. Although an American citizen, he had spent most of his life in his much loved Paris, until the war forced him to leave. He seemed unhappy and disoriented in New York and clung to his French friends there. He had known the Maritains for many years, and was very fond of them; he became a frequent visitor at 30 Fifth Avenue.

Jacques, as I said earlier, began making broadcasts to France as soon as America entered the war. In September 1943, these addresses were programed weekly and continued up to the time of the Allied landing in Normandy the following year. He spent a good deal of time on the preparation of these broadcasts, and never begrudged it in spite of the pressure of other work.

That year he published two works of his in French with the Éditions de la Maison Française and in English his *Rights of Man and Natural Law* and *Education at the Crossroads*, the latter based on a series of lectures he had just given at

Yale under the sponsorship of the Terry Foundation. Dealing with educational problems he had often discussed with Robert Hutchins and John Nef at Chicago, and supplemented by his own observations in American institutions of learning he had visited, *Education at the Crossroads* attracted considerable attention in university and other intellectual circles.

In 1943, Jacques Maritain was sixty years old. The philosophical review *The Thomist* honored him with the publication and presentation of a "Maritain Volume," containing appreciations of his work by outstanding personages in the philosophical and educational fields, both Catholic and non-Catholic. The anniversary was also marked by another celebration which I remember well. Jacques was born on November 18, 1882, but for some reason I have never been able to fathom, a group of his friends decided to hold a large "birthday luncheon" for him early in the year, on January 9, at the Waldorf-Astoria in New York. At this affair many tributes were paid Jacques by civic and religious leaders, but among the most eloquent was one by Dorothy Thompson, a moving speaker and one of the noted journalists of the war years. "Monsieur Maritain," she said, "understands America because he understands the American dream. He understands the American dream because he understands the European dream. And he understands the European dream because he understands the yearnings of humanity."

Toward the end of 1943, the Maritains of course shared with all of us a more hopeful view of the outcome of the war. Bitter fighting went on, but the events of the year had marked a turning point in the fortunes of the Allies. As early as February the German tide had ebbed in Russia; Africa had been cleared of Axis forces by May; and in September the Allies had invaded southern Italy. Throughout German-occupied Europe, underground forces, largely supplied by the Allies, had begun to harass the invaders.

But even when the war news was bleakest, the gatherings

at the Maritains' were far from cheerless affairs. Jacques could be most amusing in a gently ironic way. He liked to tease and one of his targets was Vera, who accepted this with her usual calm and amiability. She had a most expressive face, and as one of their friends said, "her silences were as articulate as Jacques's and Raïssa's conversation." Either of the two could keep a talk going with almost anyone, and quickly find a subject of interest to the listener. The food served on these occasions—again they were usually on Sunday afternoons—was very simple. There were always tea and cakes, but Jacques himself leaned to peanuts and ginger ale, which for a Frenchman of his generation were pleasantly exotic.

On the evening of December 31, 1943, Raïssa and Jacques invited a group of some twenty close friends to their home to see the New Year in. When I arrived at nine o'clock an unusually festive atmosphere already prevailed. There was animated chatter, refreshments were served, and the hours passed quickly. My most vivid remembrance of that evening is the arrival on the scene of the artist Marc Chagall, then carrying on his painting in New York and Connecticut. Exactly as the clock struck twelve, there was a loud bang as the elevator opened in the outside hall, and into the room rushed a short man with shoulder-length gray hair, a merry face, and dancing eyes, holding straight before him a large bouquet of red roses for Raïssa Maritain. They were, to a petal, the red roses that reappear, dreamlike, in his painting. Chagall soon came over to join his wife Bella and his daughter, with whom I was talking, bringing into the conversation the *joie de vivre* and touch of fantasy that are the delight of his art.

In spite of the crowded schedule in which they had become involved, the Maritains continued to carry out their religious devotions. Raïssa and Vera liked to go to the impressive Jesuit Church of Saint Francis Xavier or to the French Church of Saint Vincent de Paul on West Twenty-third Street, where their Dominican friends, Father Ducatillon and Father Couturier, occasionally preached on Sundays. When in New York, Jacques went early every morning to mass at Saint Joseph's, the parish church of Greenwich Village, close to their apartment. It was my parish church also—for from 1942 I lived on West Eleventh Street—and I frequently saw the slim, white-haired figure kneeling before the altar or passing through the street on his way from mass as I myself went to work.

Through the Maritains' influence, some of their new American friends were attracted to the Catholic Church; again they had godchildren as at Meudon. Among these were Emily Scarborough Coleman, a sensitive poet and artist, and her son John. Emily Coleman had come to know them in 1942 after reading the first volume of Raïssa's memoirs. A year later she decided to become a Catholic, and was baptized by Father Couturier at the Church of Saint Vincent de Paul; her son John had preceded her into the Church a few months earlier. Both knew French well, and Emily was especially drawn to Raïssa, and to Raïssa's concept of a contemplative life lived in the world. John became Jacques's helper on various fronts, and especially in connection with translations of his writings. John and Harry Binsse worked together on the difficult task of putting into English Raïssa's selections from the works of Léon Bloy, a large volume later published by Pantheon Books.

Another of Jacques's American godchildren was Dorothy Rothchild. She was just out of college when she met Jacques at the Catholic Worker; as she had an excellent command of French and English, she offered to help him in any way she could. For several years she acted as his secretary, helping him with his books both in New York and later at Princeton. (When in 1948 she married Dr. Pierre Brodin, one of the first professors at the École Libre, Jacques was the best man at their wedding.)

In the anxious and feverish days when Jacques realized that the Allies were preparing to invade France, he began to work on an address to the French people to be broadcast at the beginning of their liberation. He wanted to tell them that for four years he had spoken for them as best he could, and now would do so no longer. But he wished to say that no matter how serious the divisions among them, they should remember that in the motto of their Republic the most essential word was "fraternity" and that their most pressing duty was to face *together* the immense work of reconstruction. He referred to the sympathy for France that he had found everywhere among Americans, and trusted that the liberating Americans would be received with the same sympathy by Frenchmen. This fine address—to which my few words above have by no means done justice—was broadcast by the Office of War Information shortly after the Allied landing in Normandy.[2]

At this hour of emotion, long pent up and finally released, both Jacques and Raïssa were completely exhausted, almost ill, and their doctor recommended that they get out of the city for the summer. They had visited East Hampton on several occasions earlier, and now made arrangements for a three months' stay. Jacques knew that he would have to come into New York City frequently, but it was quite accessible on the train. Although they did not get the rest they had hoped for, since calls on Jacques's time mounted, they benefited from the Atlantic air at East Hampton, and Raïssa and Vera particularly appreciated the verdure and quiet of the pleasant seaside town.

The rest permitted Raïssa to finish the second volume of her memoirs, on which she had been working for over a year. Again it was published in French, as Volume Two of *Les Grandes Amitiés*, and in English as *Adventures in Grace*, and again I worked with her as I translated. The interest aroused by her first volume, and the many moving letters

[2] It was later published in a small booklet, *A Travers la Victoire* (Paris and Fribourg: Egloff, 1945).

she had received from French and American correspondents, led her to deal more fully with the spiritual lives of their great friends of early days; chronologically the book did not progress beyond the early 1920s. Raïssa intended to deal with later happenings in future memoirs, but the turn the Maritains' lives soon took made it impossible for her ever to return to this project.

The Maritains were back in their New York apartment by October, in time for Jacques to resume his lectures. They were in better health and encouraged by the prospects of an Allied victory. Paris had been liberated in August; and General de Gaulle had entered at once, bringing from London the provisional government which had already formed in Algiers. It was soon joined by new men coming out of the National Council of Resistance, among them Georges Bidault, who was a friend of Jacques's. The situation in France was still difficult; hard fighting still went on to the north and in pockets along the Atlantic coast. The country was decimated of manpower, short of fuel, food, and transportation. Worse, there were bitter rivalries among the French themselves, and the setting up of a permanent form of government to succeed the "French State" founded at Vichy seemed an infinitely complex problem.

Jacques was scarcely back in New York when it was strongly represented to him that his presence in France would be in his own and the national interest. There was pressing family business to be attended to. Jacques's mother had died in the fall of 1943; there was the question of her affairs and the welfare of his sister and niece, of the house in Meudon, and of the fate of certain of their friends. Jacques decided that he should go as soon as possible to see conditions for himself. After receiving an *"ordre de mission,"* on the night of November 10, 1944, he left for Paris on an American military plane.

IX

Ambassador to the Vatican

When, after seven weeks, Jacques returned from France on January 1, 1945, he was much depressed. He had found Paris dark, dank, and cold; the lack of housing was causing almost as much misery as the lack of food. Although black markets flourished for those who still had a bit of money, there was desperation among the poor. The food the Americans were sending had yet to arrive. Merchandise of any kind was in short supply, and the iron shutters before many shops stayed closed. When he reached Meudon, he found the house so dilapidated that he did not see how he, Raïssa, and Vera could ever go back there to live.

He had heard belatedly of deaths of friends or of their relatives, and of deportations just before the Liberation into the *Nacht und Nebel* beyond the Rhine. He learned more details of his mother's last illness and death. Living alone in her apartment with her housekeeper Thérèse, she had offered her home as a meeting place for friends in the Resistance movement, and had never wavered in her optimism as to the future of France. Up to the last she talked of Charles Péguy, of his genius and of his struggles. Among those who went to see her in her last days was a great physician, Professor Robert Debré, who as a student had first brought Péguy to her home; his son, Michel Debré, was destined to become one of de Gaulle's closest associates, a member of almost every Cabinet of the Fourth Republic, and for several years Prime Minister of the Fifth. Another frequent visitor to Jacques's mother had been the Dominican Father Raymond Bruckberger, who had in secret been chaplain of the Resistance of the Seine and, although from time to time a guest of the Gestapo, had managed to survive. He, too, told Jacques of the courage with which Madame Favre-Maritain had faced her end.

What most disturbed Jacques, he said, was the spirit that prevailed among his compatriots; his radioed plea for fraternity had borne little fruit. The Frenchmen one passed in the street walked with averted eyes and did not speak to anyone. There was bitterness and suspicion between onetime friends, and charges and countercharges of collaboration with the occupant. He said in answer to my question that personally he had fared reasonably well as to food and lodging, but had suffered most physically from the cold—as did everyone. He had worked for some weeks at the Foreign Ministry in hat, overcoat, and gloves; for on arriving in Paris he found himself involved in a way he never expected.

Georges Bidault was General de Gaulle's minister of foreign affairs, and both asked Jacques to accept the post of French ambassador to the Holy See, to succeed Léon Bérard, the Vichy ambassador, who had been removed. Jacques could not imagine himself in such a role and vigorously declined. For a while he thought the idea had been put to rest, but after a few days they came back with such insistence on his duty as a Frenchman to serve his country still at war that he succumbed. He said he was in despair as he thought of his future plans for philosophical work and the strain this change would put on Raïssa and Vera, neither of them in good health. Nevertheless, he had accepted, so the greatest part of his stay in Paris had to be spent in briefing himself on the complicated religious situation in France and the problems it posed for the provisional government.

I never heard Jacques mention what those problems were. So far as I know, he never discussed privately or publicly his official activity as ambassador, nor do we find traces of it in his writing. And, as is usual, the Vatican archives were closed for fifty years. But from other sources one knows that during the Occupation a number of the Catholic bishops had supported Vichy as the lawful government of France; especially at the beginning, this regime had passed many measures favorable to the Church. As time went on, however, many of the lower clergy and faithful had repudiated allegiance to Vichy; there was resentment against the ultraconservative members of the hierarchy on the part of priests and laymen. There was even danger of an anti-clerical backlash in liberated France and a crisis of authority within the Church itself.

After the installation of the provisional government in France, General de Gaulle had demanded the immediate departure from Paris of all diplomats who previously had been accredited to Vichy, and their replacement by others accredited to him personally. The papal nuncio, who by international conventions is dean of the diplomatic corps, was not excepted, and an embarrassed official of the Quai d'Orsay asked Monseigneur Valerio Valeri to return to Rome. The Vatican filed no formal protest, but replaced him by the then little-known apostolic delegate to Turkey, who turned out to be none other than Archbishop Angelo Roncalli, the future "Good Pope John."

Thus, when Jacques Maritain accepted his mission as ambassador of France to the Vatican, Archbishop Roncalli was already on his way to Paris as representative of the Holy See. It was between these two poles that a future solution had to be found for many Church-State problems in a country torn not only by the Occupation but by the Liberation. The provisional government had demanded that no less than thirty-three bishops resign their sees.[1] Other pressing questions were State subsidies to religious education; the rebuilding of destroyed or damaged churches; the status of Alsace, where the pre-1919 concordat with Germany still prevailed; the orientation of a new political party, the Mouvement Républicain

[1] In the end, after investigation of the charges against them, only three were removed.

Populaire (M.R.P.). Although this party bore no confessional label, it was chiefly made up of those liberal elements in the Church that had worked for social reform before the war.

A thorny problem within the Church itself was the worker-priest movement, which early came under suspicion in Rome. Both Archbishop Roncalli and Jacques Maritain were known to have expressed sympathy with the generous ideals of this new experiment in the apostolate to workers, and so long as either remained at his post, the movement was not impeded.[2] We do not know to what extent they worked together on this and other problems, but it is certain that in this respect their views were not unlike, for traces of Maritain's thinking are to be found in John XXIII's important encyclical *Mater et Magistra* (1961), which goes far beyond the social and economic teachings of his predecessors.

After Jacques's return to New York that New Year's Day of 1945, he had three months to fill what American commitments he could and to prepare for his departure for Rome. Raïssa and Vera could not accompany him, for the war in Europe was still going on and the only transportation was by military plane; moreover, there was much for the ladies to do in New York before they could leave. Besides closing down their apartment, they were faced with the task of purchasing supplies for the Rome Embassy and making arrange-

---

[2] The worker-priest movement was started in France shortly after the Liberation by clergy—never more than one hundred in number—who went to work individually among the de-Christianized masses as laborers themselves, living under the same conditions, sharing the same stresses. Rome feared that their irregular status, cut off from any contact with their fellow clergy, living in working-class hotels or other dubious surroundings, might cause them to become so emotionally involved with the problems of their friends the workers that instead of the workers being converted, they themselves would be influenced to defect from the Church. In a number of instances these fears proved not unfounded, and the original movement was suspended in 1954, after Archbishop Roncalli's elevation to the patriarchate of Venice. It has since been revived with more careful regulations and better preparation of the participants.

ments for them to be sent on the first ship available; they had been warned that there was nothing to be bought in Italy.

I was at 30 Fifth Avenue when Jacques departed on April 1, 1945. Going with him as his secretary was a good friend, the handsome Father Jean Cattaui de Menasce, who, being of Jewish extraction, had spent the war years in Washington as pastor of a church. His liveliness and humor that afternoon did a good deal to cheer up what might have been a most lugubrious occasion. As the two men took off, both were laughing, and Raïssa and Vera seemed to be bearing up quite well when I left their apartment.

Jacques and Father de Menasce went first to Paris, where Jacques again spent some days at the Foreign Office. They arrived in Rome on April 20 and Jacques presented his credentials on May 10. After making the acquaintance of his staff, he familiarized himself with the ambassadorial procedures and with his new duties. The French Embassy to the Holy See (which, of course, is not the French Embassy to Italy), was housed in the Palazzo Taverna, a large edifice with many rooms in the ancient Renaissance part of Rome. It seemed very empty to Jacques as he waited for over three months for Raïssa and Vera to arrive.

After many misadventures, they reached Naples on the morning of August 9. They had succeeded in embarking at Boston on the ship *Mariposa*, together with the supplies they had been advised to bring along. Jacques and Father de Menasce were on the dock in Naples to meet them, and by late afternoon they were installed in the faded elegance of the Palazzo Taverna. Raïssa later described the large reception rooms, covered with scenes from mythology painted on Cordova leather, each motif surrounded by a circle of gold; Jacques's office with its overloaded desk; her huge bedroom painted in a stiff style with biblical scenes. She was not at all overwhelmed by the grandeur of all this, and those who saw her during this time say that she filled her role as ambassadress with much grace and charm.

Postwar conditions in Rome were so miserable, perhaps even worse than in France, that there was little question of the purely social functions carried on by members of the diplomatic corps in normal times. On the other hand, the Maritains discovered much to do in the way of relief work. Desperate appeals came to the Embassy from French people stranded in Rome, and particularly from those in religious houses, long cut off from any support from their own country, and whom their Italian friends could no longer help. That first winter I had a letter from Raïssa telling of the sad condition of a group of thirty French Carmelite nuns in their convent in Rome, whom she found in rags, without heat or food, and nearly all tubercular. Was there any way that she could get aid for these enclosed contemplatives, unable to forage for themselves? The response of her American friends to whom I told of her letter was overwhelming: supplies and cash were sent to the nuns, and in response to Raïssa's appeal, published in *The Commonweal*, an avalanche of food packages continued for several years.

Although Raïssa would certainly have chosen to devote the hours to spiritual meditation and reading, she found that these relief activities and her duties as hostess at the Embassy absorbed more and more of her time. However, in the moments she could spend at her desk, she updated her book on the Patriarch Abraham and the first ages of the human moral conscience, which had been published in New York, and wrote a little book on the art of Marc Chagall. Inspired by Rome's eternal beauties, she also wrote a few short poems on such subjects as the Bridge of Sant'Angelo, the Capitoline Hill, the Roman countryside, and the mountains of Latium. Both in her diary and in letters to friends she pays tribute to the splendor of the Roman churches and to the majesty of the ceremonies.

At the Church of San Luigi dei Francesi, parish church of the French in Rome, the Maritains received a warm welcome, and shortly after Raïssa's arrival, they were presented to the French ecclesiastics at a reception held in the sacristy. At Santa Sabina, the Dominican church, Father Marie-Alain Couturier said mass for them in the little cell of Saint Dominic on Palm Sunday in 1946. Raïssa wrote how moved she was at the thought of those who had been there before them—Albert the Great, Thomas Aquinas, Catherine of Siena—and by the "gentle and discreet piety" of Father Couturier, who showed such affection and concern for the Maritain household.

In his quiet way, Jacques pursued his business with the Vatican and among the members of the Roman Curia. Some conservatives among the latter were suspicious, even hostile, toward him, but on the highest level, we are told[3] that he was warmly received and that Pope Pius XII and his deputy secretary of State, Monsignor Giovanni Battista Montini, often consulted him. With the latter, Jacques was on especially intimate terms. Monsignor Montini had spent thirty years in the Vatican Secretariate of State, and took a broad and humane view of world affairs. As a young priest, he had translated into Italian *Three Reformers*, one of Jacques's early books, and ever since had closely followed its author's writings and career. He and Jacques dined together regularly during the years the Maritains were in Rome. When, in 1954, Monsignor Montini became archbishop of Milan, he undertook to put into practice much of Jacques Maritain's social philosophy as he devoted himself to the workers and the poor of that great industrial city. Later, as Pope Paul VI, he expressed on many occasions his indebtedness to "my teacher, Jacques Maritain."

In addition to his work as ambassador, Jacques pursued as best he could his philosophical and intellectual interests. With his cultural attaché—the Dominican Father Darsy—he

---

[3] See Wladimir Ormesson, Jacques's successor as ambassador of France to the Holy See, in *Revue de Deux Mondes*, June 1973.

established at San Luigi a center where young men from the more than fifty national seminaries in Rome could meet and hold conferences. The lectures which he arranged to be given at the Centre Saint-Louis by outstanding authorities in the cultural and social fields were soon overcrowded, even though in Jacques's day they were delivered under difficulties in the basement of the church, where water seeped through the walls. (After Jacques left Rome, and when times were better, the meetings at the Center were continued by his successor in a hall large enough to hold an immense audience.)

Jacques himself resumed the lectures he had given in prewar years at the Angelicum, and wrote philosophical articles for such publications as *Nova et Vetera* and *Ecclesia*, and for American periodicals, and prefaces to the books of several friends. He also managed to produce in 1947 two short works of his own: a revision and expansion of *The Person and the Common Good*, which he put into French for publication by Desclée de Brouwer, and a new metaphysical treatise, *Court Traité de l'Existence et l'Existant*. The latter was an answer to the much discussed philosophy of existentialism which surfaced immediately after the war. Represented by Heidegger and Sartre, it rested on the premise that beyond any immediate situation there is nothing that really exists; that man is a lonely being set adrift in a meaningless universe. To such nihilistic thought, Maritain opposed "the existentialism of Thomas Aquinas," whose ontology covered a concept of the nature of being, the nature of man, and the nature of knowledge, reached through the operation of the intellect.

That same year, Jacques saw published in Paris a collection of his articles written abroad during the war, including chapters first included in books along with the work of other authors. This was the result of a visit he had received, in the fall of 1945 from Abbé Charles Journet of the University of Fribourg, an old friend and prewar co-editor at Desclée de Brouwer of the "*Questions Disputées*" series.

These wartime writings, now presented in France, had been written for such diverse readerships as that of *Liturgical Arts,* of *The Modern Schoolman,* of *The Jewish Frontier, Foreign Affairs, The Nation,* as well as of several publications in Canada and South America. Although they included a wide range of subject matter, Abbé Journet arranged them for publication in a book to be called *Raison et Raisons*[4] which, divided into three parts, presented a cross section of Jacques's preoccupations at the time. The first part contains short pieces on speculative and moral theology; the second, his replies to certain criticisms of his views on democracy, human equality, and anti-Semitism; the third refers to spiritual realities in their relation to temporal society. Jacques was grateful to have this scattered material appear in more permanent form, and the hours spent in going over the material with Abbé Journet cemented a relationship that was destined to become even closer in the future when, as Cardinal Journet, the quiet, retiring Swiss priest became an influential figure in the councils of the Church.

During the years of their Roman residence, the Maritains spent their vacations in France. They went to Paris, of course, and in the summer of 1947, to Cannes. But they most looked forward to their stays at Kolbsheim in Alsace, where they could relax in the peace and seclusion of the guest house of the hospitable Grunelius family, close to their private chapel.

Such breaks, however, were fleeting, and Jacques spent most of three years at his desk in the Palazzo Taverna, attending to the day-to-day details of his ambassadorship. He said that he became more and more discouraged at the thought of the solid philosophical volumes he had planned to write and which required long study and much reflection. Throughout his stay in Rome he had acted devotedly in the interests

[4] Later published in revised form in English as *The Range of Reason* (New York: Charles Scribner's Sons, 1952).

of France because of his immense love for his country, yet he
felt miscast in a role he had never imagined or desired. "When
they made me an ambassador, they changed my identity," he
said to a friend.

In November 1947, Jacques was asked to go as president
of the French delegation to the second general conference of
UNESCO, held in Mexico City. There he gave the opening
address in "The Possibilities for Cooperation in a Divided
World." Describing the tensions that existed in a "world pros-
trated by postwar grief, and by the leaden mantle of rival
economic, political and ideological interests," he spoke of the
spirit that should prevail in "the common work of an organization in which all cultures and civilizations must play their
part, each being animated by its own particular spirit, whether
it springs from the Latin or from the English-speaking world,
or from the Eastern or Far Eastern world, and in which
patient experimental inquiry and search after guiding rational
principles must complement one another."

In returning to Rome from Mexico that December, Jacques
made a brief stop in New York to change planes. He was met
by Dr. Harold Willis Dodds, the president of Princeton, who
had come to New York to offer him a resident professorship
at the university in case he should decide to leave his post
in Rome. Dr. Dodds specified that his invitation was for
Jacques to give in the philosophy department a graduate
course in ethics "based on the spirit and principles of Thomas
Aquinas."

The opportunity to teach the principles of Thomistic moral
philosophy in this great secular university of Presbyterian origin was particularly appealing to Jacques. At that time, however, he could give President Dodds no definite answer, but
asked for time to consider so attractive a proposal. He had to
give serious thought at this juncture to what turn his future
work should take; what was best for Raïssa and Vera; where
they should live. He said at the beginning that he would

serve as ambassador for only three years; those three years would be up the following May.

That spring Jacques sent his resignation to the French government; it was to take effect on May 10, the date he had presented his credentials at the Vatican three years before. On June 1, he was received in farewell audience by Pope Pius XII. Two weeks later, he, Raïssa, and Vera left the Palazzo Taverna and went direct to Naples, where on June 16 they boarded a ship for New York. Jacques had decided that he would teach and live at Princeton.

X

The Princeton Years

In the quiet university town of Princeton, with its wide lawns, its collegiate Gothic towers, and tree-lined streets, the Maritains were to make their home for the next twelve years. After the pressure and formalities of his official duties in Rome, Jacques returned with relief to the more congenial academic atmosphere and the preparation of lectures and books on philosophy. At the university he had at close hand unusual facilities for research, and the stimulation of contacts with teaching staff and students. Always responsive to those around him, he quickly made friends. In his *Reflections on America* he later wrote: "American people—not only institutions of learning, centers of research, or foundations, but a surprising number of individuals as well—are anxious to discover men from whom any kind of improvement in the common treasure of the mind may be expected, and to give them a helping hand, so that they can pursue their work in a way profitable to mankind."

The Maritains spent their first year at Princeton in the comfortable residence of a professor absent on sabbatical leave. They moved into it in mid-August 1948, and I remember a visit to them there one afternoon in early fall as the leaves were beginning to turn. I found the same Jacques, Raïssa, and Vera, in no way altered by the dignities of Rome. In the Maritain's friendships, time and distance never seemed to create a separation, and I was made to feel we had parted only yesterday, instead of three years before.

With the opening of the scholastic year, Jacques began his graduate course on the first concepts of moral philosophy, announced as "Systematic Ethics: Analysis of Fundamental

Attitudes." He had already written on the practical relation of the person to the common good, on the meaning of the natural moral law, and on the rights of man. These were among the subjects he incorporated into his lectures before a new audience. His students at Princeton remember the slight, white-haired figure in the dark suit who delighted them by the wry humor and serious content of his talks. While remaining within his established Thomistic framework, he pushed the thought of each statement to its edge, giving a contemporary aspect to the question, and testing his hearers' reactions. There was something genial and personal in his intellectual courtesy that made them feel that he cared about their opinions. Some of those students are now teaching philosophy themselves, and say that they learned a great deal from his methods and approach as well as from the knowledge that he imparted.

In addition to his course at Princeton, Jacques taught at Hunter College in New York, and each year went to lecture at Notre Dame and Chicago. And early in the Princeton years he embarked on a major project of his own: an extensive analysis of the history of moral thought which would reach to the root of human ethical experience, and deal with the core issues facing moral man. He envisaged this as a long-term project, and such indeed it was, for it involved examination and comparison of the moral philosophy of the East and of the West in every age. His *Moral Philosophy: An Historical and Critical Survey of the Great Systems* was not to appear in final form for a good many years, but he said that its planning was never absent from his mind.

Princeton was now the Maritains' "official" home, but as they did not have it in their hearts to break their ties with France, they planned to go abroad for at least three months each summer. For the next few years they were able to carry out this intention. In May and June 1949, Jacques opened in Paris the annual Week of French Catholic Intellectuals with a seminar on "The Roads of Faith," and spoke at the Institut Catholique on "The Meaning of Contemporary Atheism." In such ways as these he renewed his contacts with his European colleagues, and each year at some point the Maritains went to the home of the Gruneliuses at Kolbsheim.

On their return to Princeton in the fall of 1949, they moved into their own home at 26 Linden Lane. With the help of President Dodds, Jacques had made arrangements to purchase this house during the first year when the Maritains lived in quarters they knew to be temporary. The grounds surrounding their new place were small, but the cream-colored stucco building with its white wood trim had the number of rooms they needed, and was situated on a quiet side street not far from the university. Raïssa and Vera spent much care on its arrangement, and succeeded—although they did not try to bring their furniture from France—in restoring much of the same atmosphere as at Meudon. As Raïssa especially mourned the absence of the distant glimpse of Paris from their old home, their good friend André Girard, a pupil of Rouault's and himself a distinguished artist, painted a delightful Parisian scene on the walls of the new dining room, and a floral pattern on those of the living room and hall. I recall that framed on the mantelpiece of the latter was a fine painting of his, *The Flight into Egypt*, and that other walls were hung with favorite pictures, including the biblical drawings of Marc Chagall.

In my papers I find a note from Jacques saying that they were finally *almost* installed at Linden Lane, and would I come to the "inauguration" of their new home at a tea on Saturday afternoon, November 26? At this crowded and cheerful affair, I remember meeting a number of Jacques's colleagues at the university, among them President Dodds; Sir Hugh Taylor, dean of the graduate school; Professor Gilbert Chinard; and Father Quitman Beckley, chaplain of the Newman Club.

Raïssa seemed adjusted to her surroundings and more at peace, since at Princeton she was able to set aside regular hours each day for the solitude she desired. Afterward she would read over and discuss Jacques's writings with him, write occasional articles for such publications as *The Commonweal*, and follow her special interests in art and music. The composer Arthur Lourié and his wife had come to live and work in the United States, and Raïssa went to New York several times to visit them and to hear Arthur play for her his latest compositions. When overnight in New York, the Maritains often stayed with Mr. and Mrs. Robert Louis Hoguet, great admirers of theirs, who usually assembled an interesting group to meet them.

Unfortunately, in the early spring of 1950, Raïssa suffered a severe attack of shingles which lasted for six weeks and left her weak and in deteriorating health. She was afterward often confined to her room if not to her bed; at such times, she read a great deal or composed poems. She looked forward all year to her summers in France and, when able, wrote long letters to her intimates there.

In working on his books at Princeton, Jacques did not take long to assemble a corps of devoted helpers. His most constant and congenial aide was Cornelia Borjerhoff, the wife of Professor E. B. O. Borjerhoff, a specialist in European literature. Mrs. Borjerhoff acted as Jacques's research assistant and secretary for all his Princeton years. She was devoted to his interests and remained in close touch with his American affairs as long as he lived; since his death she has remained a source of helpfulness and advice to his friends. Jacques could also count on those who had aided him during the war years, and for certain of his books Dorothy Rothchild Brodin came from New York to help with translations and preparation of copy. Sundry editors, translators, godchildren, and friends often traveled the road between New York and Princeton.

The same road was frequently taken by Jacques's European

colleagues and friends when they visited the United States; he kept himself well informed of intellectual and spiritual movements abroad. Father Marie-Alain Couturier always came to see the Maritains when he was in America, keeping them in touch with the postwar work of the great French artists with whom he was associated. The Englishman Robert Speaight, a creative writer whose interests also lay in the theater (he is a distinguished actor himself), continued a friendship with the Maritains that dated back to their years at Meudon, was maintained in New York during the war, at Notre Dame University, and in Rome during Jacques's ambassadorship. When in the United States on lecture tours, he always came to Princeton, and at one point remained there for four months while he spoke at the Christian Gauss seminars on literary criticism.

In the early 1950s there came a visitor who was to be associated with Jacques in his later life in a way that, I am sure, neither of them could have expected at the time. This visitor was Father René Voillaume, the first prior of the Fraternity of the Little Brothers of Jesus, followers of Father de Foucauld. After a career as an army officer and explorer in Algiers and Morocco, Charles de Foucauld (1858–1916) became a priest, and returned to the southern Sahara to lead a life of prayer, contemplation, and service to the world's most forsaken people, the desert nomads. He had died there alone during the First World War, assassinated by fanatics when some of the tribes turned against France. During the fifteen years he lived among the Tuaregs, he longed for helpers in his work, and had drawn up a rule of life for a "double spiritual family" of Brothers and Sisters. Several isolated attempts were made to follow his example, but the seed he had sown lay fallow for many years.

In 1933, Father Voillaume, after a careful study of the writings of Charles de Foucauld, set out to form the congregation the dead priest had planned. He considered that such a work was needed more than ever, not only in Africa and other countries of the third world but in the very real wilderness of the slums of our large modern cities. So difficult and demanding is the life of the Little Brothers that it took René Voillaume fourteen years to win the Church's approval of their constitutions. The congregation of the Little Brothers of Jesus counted only fifteen members at the outbreak of the Second World War, but since that conflict it has been joined by hundreds of young men to whom this mode of service has made a strong appeal.

Because of Jacques's connection with the Brothers later on, I shall try to describe them briefly: They are religious contemplatives who lead an ascetic, prayer-centered life in the world; they take the vows of poverty, chastity, and obedience. They engage in manual labor, sharing the insecurity of the poor, accepting the humblest work, the poorest pay. They own nothing, not even the little places where they live. They rent their homes or, where none are available, build shelters for themselves; their only luxury is cleanliness. For mutual help and support, they live in groups of from three to five; one of their number is a leader responsible to the head of the congregation.

Except for a small badge—a cross surmounted by a heart—they are in no way distinguished by their dress from the laborers around them. They may not engage in convert-making activities, but must try by example, not by words, to bring charity and friendship into the lives of the disinherited and forsaken. They welcome all who come to them—for advice, for food or help in sickness, for a bit of companionship. To their homes, sparsely furnished with the bare necessities of life, they return after their work, whatever it may be, to spend prescribed hours in prayer, either alone or in common; in each Fraternity a room is always set aside as a chapel. Here they hear mass and spend a time in worship each day; at such times they wear a light gray habit over their workmen's clothes. It should be added that some of the Little Brothers are priests.

The rigorous life of the Fraternities requires a long and intensive training, since the members have to be prepared to live under the most substandard or primitive conditions, and among people of other faiths or of none. Not all temperaments are suited to this mode of life: introspective, anxiety-prone, or unstable personalities are not accepted. Each member has to spend a period of trial in a working Fraternity, followed by a novitiate of one year, a further probationary period of two years, and after that three to six years in the study of theology and philosophy. It was in connection with the last requirement that Father Voillaume came to Jacques at Princeton to discuss with him the way to organize a body of philosophical studies suitable to them.

Jacques had known Father Voillaume since the time of the foundation of the congregation he headed. He had followed with interest the impact of the new form of religious life practiced by the Little Brothers and by the similar congregation of the Little Sisters of Jesus who lived in the same way, seeing in both the answer to a great need in the materialistic postwar world. The report Father Voillaume now gave him of the growth and spread of the Fraternities touched him deeply, and for her part, Raïssa was overcome by this realization of an ideal so closely approaching her own. They invited a number of friends from New York and Princeton to meet Father Voillaume and to hear what he had to say. Those who came were impressed, and a knowledge of the Little Brothers' work was fairly well spread before any of their Fraternities were actually established in the United States. (Although the Little Sisters of Jesus came earlier, some years went by before the Brothers were convinced that there was need of their presence in "affluent" America.) After Father Voillaume's visit to Princeton, Jacques continued in touch with him, and when on vacation in Paris saw a good deal of the Little Brothers in that city.

Returning each year to the United States for the opening of the academic term, Jacques plunged at once into his teaching and writing. In 1950, he delivered at the University of Chicago the Walgreen Foundation Lectures on "Man and the State." It was some fifteen years since he had described in general terms in *True Humanism* the internal principles for the structure of a new Christendom. Since then he had extended the personalist and pluralist views expressed in that book to the desirable relationship of man to the body politic, of Church to State, and of nations to one another. In these lectures he developed at length the international dimensions of an ideal world society in which the general welfare would be the prime consideration rather than narrow national interests and absolute state sovereignty. It is commonly said that, together with *True Humanism*, these lectures in book form, published by the Chicago University Press (1951), constitute Maritain's two major contributions to political philosophy.

There was another area in which Jacques's interest never waned: the problems and psychology of the creative worker. In 1951, he gave at Princeton, under the auspices of the Council of Humanities, six conferences on "The Responsibility of the Artist." And in the spring of 1952 he was invited to deliver the first series of Mellon Lectures on the Fine Arts at the National Gallery in Washington; his subject was "Creative Intuition in Art and Poetry." As we know, Jacques and Raïssa had shared a lifelong preoccupation with the creative arts, and Jacques said several times that as a philosopher he "would not have dared to speak of poetry if he could not rely on the direct experience of a poet"; it was in this connection that Raïssa had always made her most immediate contribution to her husband's writing.

The six lectures in Washington were to be illustrated by

slides, and a choice had to be made of great paintings of
East and West, ancient and modern; here Jacques needed
examples available to everyone, and in this the staff of the
National Gallery gave valuable assistance. To point out the
distinctions and relationship between art and poetry, those
"two strange companions," he selected quotations principally
from the works of French, British, and American writers. In
choosing the latter two, he had the help of Francis Fergusson,
director of the seminars in literary criticism at Princeton, and
for American examples the advice of the poet and critic
Allen Tate.

Jacques and Mrs. Borjerhoff toiled for endless hours as
Jacques combined their research in support of a philosophical
thesis based on the aesthetics of Aristotle and Aquinas, in
which he emphasized the role of the intellect, as well as of
the imagination, in poetic and artistic activity. The lectures
were widely discussed, and appeared the following year in a
handsomely illustrated volume published by the Bollingen
Foundation and Pantheon Books.

Jacques's appointment to the Princeton philosophy department ended in 1952. He stayed on in what he described
as the "Elysian status" of professor emeritus, a presence in
Princeton—physically, intellectually, and spiritually. Various
students who had followed his course continued to come to
him for advice and guidance; he remained in touch with
members of the university faculty and with such scholars
as Albert Einstein and Robert Oppenheimer at the Institute
for Advanced Study. But he could now spend more and more
time on his writing, and although he lectured at the university
only occasionally after his retirement, he filled his annual
engagements in the universities of the Middle West as long as
he lived in America.

Tragedy struck at Linden Lane when, in March 1954,
Jacques was felled by a severe heart attack. For more than
two months he was completely immobilized. He tells that

during those seemingly endless weeks the events of his personal life floated before him "filled in by details and reflections to which a dreamlike state lent an illusory interest." Actually, he considered that Raïssa with her capacity for total recall had already written in her memoirs of the essentials of their early lives and he still hoped that she could bring her recollections up to date. Nevertheless, he decided that he should go over his own papers and notes to set down "certain information on the exterior facts and debates with which the events of our lives were connected." This was the genesis of his *Carnet de Notes,* on which he began to work the following fall; but he did not complete it until 1965 and, due to intervening events, in a form quite different from the one he had planned at first.

During his illness, Jacques was surrounded by the concern and attentions of his friends. When I went down to see them, Raïssa spoke tearfully of the proofs of affection showered on Jacques during his ordeal. Closest to them at the time were the families of two of Jacques's colleagues, Professor Luigi Crocco, an aeronautical engineer, and Professor Jean Labatut, a noted architect and teacher of architecture. And from that time forward the Maritains had the aid of Jane Somerville, who had first come to them as a seamstress, but remained as helper, nurse, and friend in difficult days thereafter.

Jacques was up and around by the following summer, but his doctor decreed that he remain at Princeton under observation, so there could be no question of the annual European hegira. By fall he was better, but his heart was to be seriously affected for the rest of his life. He resumed his activities, saw his friends, and extended help to others as he had always done. I recall that in the spring of 1955 he became much interested in Abbé Pierre, the "ragpicker priest." A man of wealthy background, Henri Grouès had been a deputy in the French Parlement from 1946 to 1951, when he gave up

all comfort and all political life to work with the population
of down-and-outers who ever since François Villon have
been a part of Paris folklore, and also the despair of its social
workers and police. Known only as Abbé Pierre, he organized
and himself lived at "Emmaus," a village of lean-to huts
made of rubble and tin cans, with a flock of derelict men
who drew a pitiful subsistence from the rags and metals of
the vast trash dumps on the eastern edge of Paris. In the
dreadful cold of January 1954, several homeless people who
had not found the refuge of Emmaus were frozen to death,
and the Abbé passed into action. The Paris public answered
his dramatic appeals generously, but in the emergency of the
still-existing postwar housing shortage, the Abbé turned for
further funds to the generosity of Americans and—speaking
not a word of English himself—to the Maritains.

Jacques invited to Princeton a number of his friends to
meet the French priest and to offer what suggestions they
could. Among them was Marshall Suther, a former pupil of
his at Columbia University, whom he enlisted to act as interpreter and to accompany the Abbé through the States on a
fund-raising tour. Human misery always touched Jacques and
Raïssa deeply, and I remember that after the meeting at
Princeton, Raïssa went to her room and returned with a box
of jewelry, including her father's gold watch, which she
quietly put into the Abbé's hands as he left.[1]

In May of 1955, a few months after Abbé Pierre's visit, the
Maritains sailed for France on the French liner *Liberté*. They
spent two weeks in Alsace, and the rest of the time in Paris
at an apartment on the rue de Varenne, placed at their dis-

[1] It should be noted that, in the long run, efforts such as Abbé Pierre's
galvanized the French government, which has now demolished most of the
slum areas of the big French cities and realized a vast campaign of low-cost
housing. An excellent account of the Abbé's work, *Abbé Pierre and the
Ragpickers of Emmaus*, was written by French journalist Boris Simon, and
an English translation was published on the eve of the Abbé's arrival in
America in 1955 by P. J. Kenedy & Sons.

position by Madame Grunelius. From there Jacques fanned out to renew his contacts in intellectual and publishing circles, and Raïssa and Vera received their old friends. The otherwise pleasant vacation was marred, however, by a mishap when Raïssa was knocked down in the street by a motorcyclist. Although no bones were broken, she was sore and bruised and had to remain in bed for several weeks. Actually, Vera, who was with her sister at the time of the accident, was more permanently affected, for she had been terribly frightened and unnerved.

For poor Vera this was the last trip to France; in 1956, she had a heart attack and some months later there appeared the symptoms of cancer. All plans now revolved around her, as for the next three years she battled the fatal disease. In their turn, Jacques and Raïssa had to mount guard over the one who so long had cared for them and protected them from the small daily worries of life as though they were her children. In a touching chapter of his *Carnet de Notes*, Jacques writes of Vera's fortitude and self-sacrificing character and describes the course of her illness, its progress and remissions. Only once, at East Hampton, in the summer of 1957, was Vera well enough to take up for a short time her usual household duties when medical reports, based on X rays, encouraged them to believe that she was completely cured.

With hope restored, Jacques and Raïssa wrote together that summer at East Hampton a small book on two subjects close to their hearts: *Liturgy and Contemplation*. At a time when new stress was being placed on the communal aspects of worship and the activist role of the Church, they wished to remind their fellow Catholics that liturgy and contemplation could not be opposed to one another. True participation in liturgical ceremonies and offices required that prayer in common and in the name of all be combined with a personal relationship and union with God; this was cultivated in "private" prayer and meditation. Their book stressed the need of contemplatives, not only in religious orders, but among lay persons who remain faithful to contemplative prayer while continuing to live in the ordinary circumstances of family and social life. It is, I believe, the best key to the spiritual ideals which the Maritains tried all their lives to attain themselves.

That same summer Jacques began to put together his engaging and perceptive *Reflections on America*, based on three seminars he had held the previous fall for students at the University of Chicago under the auspices of the Committee on Social Thought. He had enjoyed the informal discussions with young people who had brought their perplexities to him, enlightening him still further on some of our national idiosyncrasies. He had not intended writing a book along these lines, but on the insistence of Dr. John Nef, Jacques put aside for a while the writing of a paper on the philosopher Hegel to give his impressions of the American character and attitudes.

In his testimony to the idealism and generosity of Americans, their concern for moral and religious values, their eagerness for knowledge, Jacques showed his love for our country, its people, and its institutions. At the same time he entered into a frank discussion of certain of our national deficiencies and illusions. While he considered Americans as the least materialist of modern people who have reached the industrial stage, he remarked on the mandatory importance they attached at that time to business success, on the low esteem accorded artists and intellectuals, on the defects of American education, on race prejudice, and on a proneness to think of problems of human love in simple terms of sex. In a chapter on "Marriage and Happiness," he warns of the American tendency to consider marriage as both the perfect fulfillment of romantic love (based on sexual desire) and the pursuit of full individual self-realization. Romantic love, he said, was desirable in every marriage, at least at the start, but it had to be transmuted into something deeper—more human, more personal, and disinterested—if disillusion was not to result.

As elsewhere in his writings, Jacques expressed in this book his admiration for the American political system, saying that it is "in my opinion the best conceived and the most efficient (at least in the long run) among all democratic regimes . . . precisely because it demands from men a perpetual effort to surmount its imperfections, and to keep it working, and to keep improving it." Written in the informal style in which he discussed these matters with the Chicago students, *Reflections on America*, published in 1958, turned out to be one of Jacques Maritain's most popular books.

As Vera's condition worsened, Jacques spent as much time at home as he could. In 1958, he went to lecture at Chicago, and then to Notre Dame for the inauguration of the Maritain Center; that year he gave a lecture at Princeton in honor of the centenary of Bergson's birth; he attended a few important conferences in New York and Philadelphia. But often now he was in consultation with physicians in Princeton and New York, taking Vera back and forth to doctors' offices and hospitals for treatment, trying at first to hide from Raïssa the hopelessness of the outlook, then having to tell her the truth. She accepted the doctors' verdict with fortitude and, although by now there were nurses around the clock, spent her own days hovering over her sister. Toward the end, Vera's suffering was so atrocious that she was kept almost constantly under drugs. Neither Jacques nor Raïssa would hear of her being taken to a hospital, for they knew that their presence was her only human comfort. Vera died on December 31, 1959, and two days later was buried in the little cemetery adjoining the Catholic church in Princeton.

Jacques had to witness Raïssa's grief in addition to bearing his own. The two sisters had been so close together all their lives that Raïssa could not imagine life without Vera. Her own health had shattered under the strain, and she was slow to regain her strength. When summer came, however, she was able to enter into plans for the trip to France that they had forgone for several years. She was almost cheerful as she and Jacques set out, looking forward to reunion with their old friends in surroundings dear to them.

Arriving in Paris, on July 7, 1960, they went to the little Hotel de Bourgogne on the Place du Palais Bourbon, behind the Chamber of Deputies. As Raïssa passed through the door of her room she fell, stricken by a cerebral thrombosis. Now began what, I am sure, was the most sorrowful ordeal of Jacques Maritain's life.

XI

The Evening Sacrifice

Raïssa was not to recover. The doctors could not help her, for each time one phase of her illness was controlled, another appeared. For the first several months she was walled within herself by aphasia, and although she surmounted this through medical therapy and her strength of will, there followed a necessary operation on her teeth which made it difficult for her to speak. Unable to take food without nausea, she grew weaker day by day, and much of the time she was unconscious.

In the first days of her illness in her small room at the hotel where they went on their arrival in Paris, Jacques found himself in a desperate situation. Assistance came from the Little Brothers of Jesus, and when word of the Maritains' plight reached Kolbsheim, their good friend Antoinette Grunelius came to their aid. She arranged again to put at their disposition the apartment she had on the rue de Varenne, and nursing help was obtained. The Maritains had the privacy of these comfortable quarters as long as Raïssa lived, but Jacques had another trial to bear. He could seldom be with Raïssa, for when he came into her room, she made such efforts to talk to him that she became agitated, and the doctors advised him to limit his visits. So for the most part, he stayed in an adjoining room, listening to sounds, easily alarmed by every movement he heard, rarely leaving the apartment except to go to mass. His only salvation was to work as hard as he could—writing, correcting the proofs of his books.

I went to see him one afternoon in mid-October. On my arrival in Paris from the Frankfurt Book Fair, my brother told me of the sad situation on the rue de Varenne. When I telephoned, Jacques asked me to come the next day, although he explained that Raïssa was allowed no visitors. I found him sitting at his desk, an enormous pile of proofs before him. He was completely calm as he told me that, after hoping for a long time for Raïssa's recovery, he now accepted the fact that she could not live. He spoke of the kindness of their friends, of the help he had received from the Little Brothers, and of one visitor who had been permitted to see Raïssa a few days before. This was Pierre Van der Meer, who, after the death of his wife Christine, had returned to the abbey of Oosterhout to become a Benedictine and had been ordained a priest at the age of seventy-six. He had come from Holland to see Raïssa, and his visit had given Jacques great personal comfort.

Some two weeks later Raïssa received the last sacraments from the hands of Father Michel Riquet, who had been a student of Jacques's in the far-off days when he taught at the seminary at Versailles. Raïssa was entirely conscious at the time, had followed the priest's prayers and movements with attention, and afterward thanked him with a smile. After two days passed in peace and silence, she went to eternity on November 4, 1960.

Jacques was quite composed during the funeral ceremonies that followed, and as he accompanied Raïssa to her last resting place in the little village cemetery at Kolbsheim in Alsace. The Grunelius family made the necessary arrangements, and Antoinette and Alexandre Grunelius were at Jacques's right hand in the following days as he came to a fuller realization of his loss. With Vera and Raïssa both gone, he said that he had survived even himself.

He was so physically exhausted, and suffering so much with his heart, that his friends feared for his own life. After a few weeks of rest, however, he recovered his strength, and turned to the decisions that confronted him. Chief among them, of course, was where and how he would spend the rest of his days. There is no doubt that for some time in the back of his mind was the idea that he might go to Toulouse to the study center of the Little Brothers of Jesus. As we know, Father Voillaume had already asked for his help, and now he invited Jacques to make his home with them as a lay adviser on their philosophical studies. He no longer had to face the great expenses he had in the past, and felt little need for money—in fact, he had never wanted it except for the sake of those he loved. He said that, insofar as possible, his only desire was to live in retirement and to complete his unfinished philosophical work.

But first he had to attend to certain practical matters, for he wished to rid himself of material possessions. The house at Meudon he turned over to the artist Gino Severini, who was using it as a studio. With Madame Grunelius' help, he disposed of the furniture from Meudon that after the Occupation had been moved to her Paris apartment; the rest was sent to Kolbsheim, where it was placed in the guest house along with books and papers already there, and always held at his disposition.

At the end of the year, Jacques started for Princeton "to clean out his desk" on Linden Lane. It was a sad return to this house of many memories, and Jacques could not bear to turn it over to strangers. He therefore asked Arthur and Ella Lourié to occupy it as long as either lived; after that, it was to be given to Notre Dame University for the benefit of certain projects being carried on at its Maritain Center.

On January 25, a snowy, icy day, Jacques came up from Princeton to New York. As he was to sail for France the following morning, he went to a hotel close to the French Line pier. Despite the weather, he had accepted an invitation to dine that night with Mr. and Mrs. Robert Hoguet. Louise Hoguet phoned me saying that Jacques had suggested that I join them, but asked that no others be present except her family. Their son fetched Jacques from the hotel, and the dinner passed very pleasantly; Jacques became almost his old self in that friendly and cheerful atmosphere. Alas, the evening ended in tragedy, for shortly after we went up to the drawing room for coffee, Robert Hoguet had a massive heart attack. A doctor and a priest were summoned, but arrived only as he was drawing his last breath. Jacques and I remained as long as we could be of help. After I located a taxi in the snow, I left him at his hotel, sorrow and exhaustion clearly visible on his face.

*

On his return to France, he went immediately to Toulouse. Once there, the wisdom of the decision he had made became clear. He, who had never had children, soon discovered that he was the father of some sixty devoted sons, who surrounded him with affection and solicitude. Soon after his arrival at Toulouse, he wrote to André Girard: "I do not need to tell you with what marvelous charity the Little Brothers have adopted me. They are really at ease, in friendship and in freedom—a real evangelical freedom."

In the outgoing companionship of "Father Voillaume's boys," Jacques became younger and healthier. His friend Stanislas Fumet gives this impression of him at the time: "Even if after Raïssa's death, he called himself *le vieux Jacques*, his mind was no less vigorous, his clear gaze no less penetrating, his irony no less pungent, his optimism no less lively than it had been before, and this period of his life brought him something else: a supplement of freedom."

The Little Brothers' seminary for theological and philosophical training (there were, in addition, several working Fraternities in Toulouse) was on Avenue Lacordaire, a dusty road in a working-class suburb of Toulouse not far from the huge, barrack-like building that housed the provincial headquarters of the Dominicans from whom the Little Brothers drew their professors of theology. Their own quarters were a short distance away in small wooden cabins that they built themselves; their chapel when Jacques first went to them was a converted barn. In the front part of one of the cabins was a common room where meetings and classes were held. Behind this room, Jacques had his monastic lodging, two cell-like rooms with wooden walls; one was a bedroom, the other a study furnished with bookshelves and a desk; adjoining the latter was a little lavabo. To one of the other cabins a few paces away Jacques usually went to take his meals with three or four of the Brothers, saving him from the burden of loneliness.

Jacques gave the same careful preparation to the seminars he held for his little flock at Toulouse that had marked his teaching in great European and American institutions. Among his hearers were young men of vastly different origins and educational backgrounds. Some were graduates of great universities, others had only the technical knowledge gained in the practice of a craft. To bring his talks within their requirements, he spoke in informal style and updated his earlier lessons as he dealt with the great philosophical questions that men must face in every age and in every part of the world.

In May 1962, Jacques gave three seminars on "God and the Permission of Evil." He considered it particularly important for his hearers to have a good understanding of a problem on which he himself had reflected all his life, for they would be brought into contact with the contemporary forms of atheism: especially the militant atheism of Marxists and the atheism of the existentialists who competed with Marxism. In following and developing the teaching of Aquinas that there is no first principle of evil in the universe, although there is the first principle of good, he taught that God *knows* evil through the good of which evil is the privation but he does not have the *idea* or invention of it. It is in man, the creature, to whom God has given liberty and free will, that the first cause of moral evil (in the order of non-being or nothingness) is to be found. Neither is the evil of nature, or suffering, caused by the will of God, but it is admitted by him, the first cause of good in the material universe, because it is inevitably linked by nature *per accidens* to the good or gain in question—"no generation without corruption, no life without some destruction, nor any passage to a superior form of life without some death."

These seminars, which went into the subject in far more detail than I have suggested, were published in book form in France not long after they were given, and in English a few years later.[1] Jacques considered this book, together with his earlier *Existence and the Existent* (dealing with other points of the same problem), as his most important contribution to the extension of Thomistic thought.

Other seminars that Jacques gave to the Little Brothers in Toulouse are contained in a volume published shortly after his death.[2] It includes some of his most forceful and limpid writing, and reveals his preoccupations both as a philosopher and as a man of faith. In dealing with challenges to the contemporary human conscience, he is careful throughout to make clear the distinction between philosophy and theology. He does not agree with the new "transcendental Thomism" of theologians who hold Christian philosophy as a kind of "anonymous theology." Theology, he points out, is based on divine revelation which teaches certain truths, even philosophical truths, given once and for all (new dogmatic definitions "simply make explicit and complete the old ones; they don't change them in any way"). Philosophy, on the other hand is essentially *rational* knowledge, free in its own field; it calls for constant progress and development. What is needed in Christian philosophy, Maritain says, are renewals in approach and method, a freer manner of positing and treating problems,

---

[1] *God and the Permission of Evil.* Trans. by Joseph W. Evans (Milwaukee: Bruce Publishing Co., 1966).
[2] *Approches sans Entraves* (Paris: Fayard, 1973).

one more mindful of experience, the history of thought, and the developments of science. In other words, more necessary than ever is the realism of Thomas Aquinas, "whose wisdom is always young, for, on condition that his disciples do not sleep, it is renewed from age to age in the mysterious and rejuvenating fountain of truth."

Quite apart from their philosophical and humanist content, many passages in this book remind one of what a fine writer Jacques really was. This was recognized in France when, as a man of letters, he received the Grand Prize of Literature from the French Academy in 1961 and the French National Prize for Letters in 1963. He received these late honors with mixed emotions, for he said he knew what pleasure they would have given Raïssa, and she was no longer there for him to share them with her.

Jacques never recovered from Raïssa's loss. Often as he was engaged in writing, he would stop to think what she would have said on the subject; she was constantly in his thoughts. On the walls of his small, bare room he had placed photographs of her. His desk was almost a little shrine, for on it he kept his two favorite pictures of Raïssa, and every day he went out to get fresh flowers to set before them. He came to feel her invisible presence, and in conversation with others referred to what she would have said or done as though she were still alive. Something had happened early in his stay at Toulouse that quickened even more his memories of her, something that occupied his thoughts for quite a time to come.

In the summer of 1961, Jacques left the stifling heat of the valley of the river Garonne for the cool climate of Alsace and for the home among its forests that he had been made to feel was his at any time. Each day he walked up and down the yew-bordered paths of the Gruneliuses' splendid gardens that had given Raïssa what she once described as "the joy of the eyes"; each day he went to the cemetery and sat long hours by Raïssa's grave. One afternoon, as he sadly returned, Antoinette Grunelius put into his hands a great bundle of notebooks and papers—Raïssa's last bequest which she had left in the keeping of this faithful friend.

Jacques was completely taken by surprise. Of course he was aware that for many years Raïssa had kept a journal which she guarded from all other eyes, but as she had made clear that it chiefly concerned her intimate spiritual experiences, he thought it probable that she had destroyed it. Jacques now found before him a number of little diaries, kept in different years, although by no means in all, since there had been periods when it had been impossible for Raïssa to keep significant records of any kind. In addition to the notebooks, labeled by date, there were a number of large envelopes on which was written: "To keep, perhaps," or "For Jacques to look over." In these envelopes he found masses of memoranda, little essays or thoughts on spiritual subjects, or outlines for further developments of these. As Jacques went over these papers, he was overwhelmed by what they brought back of their lives together, and especially by the light they cast on Raïssa's preoccupation with the spiritual world.

Fragmentary as were these records, and despite the gaps in chronology, Jacques decided that he could find a way to share with those who had known Raïssa this moving record of a fervent religious life carried on under exceptional circumstances. To put it together with clearly indicated explanatory notes of his own and to add an adequate preface required hours of his time, but it brought Raïssa closer, and for some months it seemed that it became Jacques's paramount interest. At the end of a year, he had *Raïssa's Journal* privately printed in 250 copies which he sent to their friends. Their reaction was immediate, and on every side Jacques was urged to make the *Journal* public. In preparing a new edition to be issued by Desclée de Brouwer, Jacques was able to add other writings of Raïssa's that he had not examined earlier, and to expand the volume considerably. Then he began to work with translators for an English edition; this took years and has appeared only recently in the United States under the imprint of Magi Books (1974).

Jacques came back on a visit to Princeton in the fall of 1962, and I had the pleasure of seeing him several times there or in New York. The Louriés were now installed at 26 Linden Lane, and he felt very much at home with these old friends. He decided to give a "little party" on October 28, and I received a note asking me to come. If so, would I get in touch with André Girard, who would drive me down? Needless to say I accepted, and when André Girard drew up before my apartment house, I was surprised to see Jacques sitting in the car, for he had attended a meeting in New York the night before.

Both Jacques and André Girard were in high spirits as we sped down the New Jersey highway, and Jacques looked in better health than I had seen him for years. I recall that somehow we got on the subject of Père Teilhard de Chardin, whose writings, published since his death, were creating quite a ripple. Jacques observed mildly that he had known Père Teilhard and had great admiration for him personally, but he did not think of him as a metaphysician or a theologian, but as a scientist and a poet. This came back to me some years later when I read in Jacques's controversial *Peasant of the Garonne* a much more severe and explicit criticism of Teilhard's cosmological synthesis in which Maritain gave reasons for the opinion which has so distressed the partisans of Teilhard.

The gathering that afternoon at Princeton included some of Jacques's close friends and a few Princeton students who had asked to meet him; he was obviously pleased that they had come, and spent a good deal of time talking to them. A few days later, I paid another visit to Linden Lane. Jacques asked me to come back to go over with him some English translations of *Raïssa's Journal* which he had brought with him. We spent an afternoon looking over the pages of the enormous manuscript and discussing the terminology the translator had employed. Jacques feared that, in an effort for literary effect, the precise meaning had not been given to Raïssa's language in referring to her mode of silent prayer and absorption in God, and he insisted on inserting full explanations of what she meant by *oraison* and *recueillement*. In fact, in all this he appeared more concerned with the translations of Raïssa's writings than he had ever been with his own.

In late September of the following year I was in Paris when I received a printed reproduction of Jacques's handwriting to the effect that, due to the state of his health, he had to cease all correspondence with his friends in order to devote himself to absolutely indispensable work. At the bottom of his note, however, was another message in his own hand, written a few days earlier at Kolbsheim, saying that he would be passing through Paris within the week, and would I meet him at the Hotel Lutetia for luncheon and a talk.

When we met—it was on October 3, 1963—I found him looking very tired, and although there were flashes of his old humor, he had obviously failed a great deal since I had seen him last at Princeton. In our long conversation that day we discussed Raïssa's *Notes on the Lord's Prayer* (which I had translated for publication by Kenedy in New York) and a number of other subjects. Among them was his feeling that Catholic philosophers were turning away from the systematic Thomism that he taught, and that even among Thomists were appearing trends with which he could not agree in substance. As for the Church, he placed great hope in the renewal of spiritual life that should be brought about by the Second Vatican Council which, after the death of Pope John, had recently been reconvened by Pope Paul VI. Jacques also spoke of the trouble he was still having with his heart, requiring him to take a number of hours of rest each day. Otherwise, he said, he was content with his present life. He was where he wanted to be—at Toulouse—with good and humble men whom he loved and trusted and in surroundings where he could write and have time "to make his soul."

As I left him that day, I wondered if I would ever see this good friend again. It was, in fact, my last meeting with Jacques, although I had letters and messages from him through May 1969. His recuperative powers were enormous —or was it sheer strength of will?—for between our last meeting and his death he had published more books, crossed to Princeton one more time, and was present in Rome for the closing session of the Second Vatican Council.

In following the published reports of the progress of the Council, I often thought how mistaken Jacques had been in thinking that the influence of his teachings had come to an end. The deliberations in Rome showed how deeply many of his central themes had pervaded the Catholic consciousness of his time. Many of them were new enough when he first became their advocate. One could cite as examples: the importance of ecumenism and religious liberty, the dignity and rights of the human person, fraternal feeling for the Jewish people and their exculpation from the age-old charge of deicide, the highlighting of the status of the laity, the recognition of the values of science, art, and democracy.

It was common knowledge that Pope Paul VI had long followed Maritain's thought and had a warm personal regard for him. Shortly after my last meeting with Jacques, and while the Council was in session, a rumor went about that the Pope had wanted to make Maritain a lay cardinal,[3] and had even made the nomination *in petto* (i.e., in secret).

---

[3] In earlier times, especially during the Renaissance, a cardinal was not necessarily a priest, yet for centuries it had been customary for only ordained men to be made cardinals. In modern times there had been only one or two exceptions—in the nineteenth century.

I do not know how this rumor started, but it was widely spread in the United States. From the Trappist monastery of Gethsemane in Kentucky, I had a letter from Thomas Merton (now Father Louis) saying that all Maritain's friends should pray and work that he might receive this honor for the good of the Church. I had to reply that I knew nothing of the matter, but that judging from my last conversation with Jacques, I thought that he would have asked to be excused from accepting this dignity, due to his often stated desire to live in retirement. Like myself, most of Jacques's close friends in France think that the red hat was not actually offered him.

In any case, it is true that he was consulted privately on certain decisions of the Vatican Council, notably on religious liberty and on Schema XIII, which defines the relations of the Church and the modern world. Pope Paul called himself "a disciple of Maritain," and in the encyclical *Populorum progressio* was to cite him along with the Fathers of the Church. Jean d'Hospital, for twenty years the Rome correspondent of the important Paris daily *Le Monde*, in describing Pope Paul's daily routine, writes: "Before going to sleep, he reads a few pages of the Gospels, or of Saint Augustine, or of Jacques Maritain. These are his bedside books."

Jacques was especially invited to Rome for the closing days of the Second Vatican Council in December 1965. At its last session, held in Saint Peter's Basilica on December 7, there came a historic moment with the reading out of a joint statement by the Pope and the Orthodox Patriarch of Constantinople, Athenagoras I. In this, the heads of both Churches declared an end to the break which had poisoned their relations for almost a thousand years; they wished, moreover, to extend an invitation to the entire Christian world to seek the ultimate unity desired by Christ. When Metropolitan Meliton of Heliopolis, the representative of Patriarch Athenagoras, came forward to receive the brief formally annulling the papal sentence of excommunication against the eleventh-century Patriarch Caerularius, he was embraced by the Pope in a kiss of peace. This was the final gesture of a movement of fraternal charity and reconciliation, of which Jacques Maritain and Nicolas Berdiaeff had been the precursors in the early 1930s. In his closing address at this session, Pope Paul paid specific tribute to the modest layman, "the great Christian philosopher Maritain," who, he said, had been one of the strongest influences in decades in religious revival among intellectuals.

The solemn ceremony of the closing of the Council was held the following day, December 8, a day of brilliant midwinter sun. For us who were not there, journalists and television have preserved the image of the innumerable throng that filled Saint Peter's Square between the embracing arms of Bernini's colonnade. Mass was to be celebrated by the Pope at an altar surmounting a platform built before the great central door of the basilica. Coming from the Vatican, the great procession of Council Fathers advanced through a long lane protected by movable barriers within which stood a cordon of uniformed Knights of Malta. There were over two thousand cardinals, bishops, and abbots, six abreast, each wearing a plain linen miter, all white above their white, black, brown, or yellow faces. It was perhaps the last great ceremonial of the Church à l'italienne, with the Pope borne above the heads of the crowd on the sedia gestatoria, between the great fans of ostrich feathers, amid the blare of silver trumpets and the huzzas of the irrepressible Roman public.

At the offertory of the mass, Cardinal Tisserant, dean of the Sacred College of Cardinals, distributed five gifts of money to show the Church's renewed concern for human welfare. The most important gift of $30,000 was toward the reconstruction of the hospital in Bethlehem. The second gift of $20,000 was to an Argentine bishop for the sectors of his diocese confided to the Little Brothers of Jesus. In the course of the liturgy, the Pope gave communion to a small group of children coming from the five continents of the world.

Finally, to climax the ceremony, seven conciliar messages were read, addressed to seven groups intended to include all categories of the human family whom the Council had tried to reach. These messages were, in order: to heads of governments; to intellectuals; to artists; to women; to the sick and the poor; to workers; to the young. The text of each message was read aloud "to the city and to the world" by a different cardinal, who then returned the document to the Pope to be presented by him to a representative of each of the seven groups. Cardinal Liénart of Lille was selected to read the Message to Intellectuals, and it was our friend Jacques Maritain who had been chosen to receive it from the head of the Church.

He was among a small company asked to stand near the Pope, and amid all the glory of the ecclesiastical vestments around him, he was wearing the humble gray habit of the Little Brothers of Jesus. (This was a sort of prediction, for he did not become a member of their congregation until four years later.) As he advanced toward the papal throne to receive the Message to Intellectuals, all saw the special emotion with which Paul VI leaned forward to receive him as he placed the document in his hands.

XII

The Peasant of the Garonne

Some months before the closing session of the Second Vatican Council there appeared in a Paris review, *La Nation Française*, an article headed: "What Does Maritain Think?" In what followed, the writer, Louis Salleron, asked specifically: "What does Maritain think of the Council? What does he think of the leading theologians of our day? What does he think of Teilhard de Chardin?"

When these questions were asked what Jacques Maritain had been thinking on such subjects for the past six years was virtually unknown. In retiring to Toulouse, he had expressed "a great thirst for silence"; any opinions he had formed on current theological trends he had kept to himself, at least so far as the public was concerned. Whether or not Salleron's article had anything to do with the book that Jacques decided to write shortly after the closing of the Council, he did not say. But on his return to Toulouse from Rome, he set down on paper the first lines of his controversial *Peasant of the Garonne*.

This epithet that he applied to himself at the age of eighty-four is significant. It is a turn of a familiar French phrase, "a peasant from the Danube," meaning a somewhat gruff, outspoken man. Jacques was writing, he said, as neither a philosopher nor a prophet, but as one who wanted to maintain the center of gravity indispensable to both: the common sense of a peasant, of one who was not afraid "to call a spade a spade." In this enigmatic book, written with all the fire of his earliest days, he warned that he would speak bluntly, and this he certainly did.

For all that the Council had finally done and decreed, he said, he was profoundly grateful, but while its sessions were in progress he had been mightily disturbed by the efforts of widely followed theologians who, in a desire to prove themselves modern, were disorienting the Christian conscience and the life of faith. While he continued to express his immense faith in human ability to make progress, he could not believe that man's essential nature had been changed by new discoveries in science and technology. "The telephone and the radio," he wrote, "do not prevent man from having two arms, two legs, two lungs, from falling in love and searching for happiness." This happiness was to be reached through a recognition of the compatibility—not the opposition—of faith with knowledge and reason.

The neo-modernists, Maritain maintained, sought to invert the announced teachings of the Vatican Council to adapt the Church to the world in a way that would bring about a complete temporalization of Christianity. The old Church was dead or dying, they said, because it had been stained by history or had alienated men from themselves; they must help reconstruct another Church, a religion of pure exaltation, a God incorporated into visible things, a Church that would be a vital force in reconstructing the world. While it was true, Jacques held, that the Christian had the duty of carrying on an unceasing struggle against the evils of social and racial injustice, starvation, destitution, and war, "nevertheless this struggle is not our one and only duty on earth because the earth and the earthly life are not the one and only reality. This temporal duty, moreover, is really and truly accomplished by the Christian only if the life of grace and prayer makes natural energies more pure and upright in the very order of nature."

Those who considered the *aggiornamento* (work of updating) effected by the Council as an adaptation of the Church to the world were mistaken. In offering her assistance

to the human race in advancing toward temporal goals for
the common good, she was but expressing in more profound
and explicit terms great truths always inherent in the evangelical teaching. This had nothing to do with the "pseudo-
scientific and pseudo-philosophical claptrap" of the neo-modernists who would have Christians depart from spiritual truths
to genuflect before new discoveries and graphs of the human
condition. Agreement on practical points with non-Christians
in today's pluralist society for the advancement of science,
culture, and education, and in the cause of true peace, did
not require Christians to change their philosophical and religious convictions.

Maritain then struck out against the phenomenological
method and form criticism of those who were trying to explain away Judaeo-Christian beliefs regarding the origin of
the world, original sin, the distinction between nature and
grace, the resurrection of the body, and immortal life, and
to interpret the cross and redemption of the historical Christ
as the sublimation of ancient myths and sacrificial rites.

In the section on "Teilhard and Teilhardism"—a small
part of the book but one that seemed to get the most attention, for by this time Père Teilhard had many enthusiastic
disciples—Maritain pays respect to the dead scientist's zeal
for truth, his painful research in the face of unwarranted
obstacles placed in his path, and sees in Teilhard's fertile ideas
and lofty aspirations "a poetic intuition—extremely powerful—of the sacred worth of created nature." Yet in Teilhard's
attempt to equate the universe in evolution with a cosmic
Christ, Maritain considered that an idea was being advanced
in which science, faith, mystique, and philosophy were in-
extricably confused.

The result of such teachings, he said, was to make a great
myth of the universal reality in an effort which Teilhard
himself described as to "establish within me, and spread
around me, a new religion (let us call it, if you like, a better

Christianity) in which the personal God ceases to be the great neolithic proprietor of old in order to become the soul of the World which our religious and cultural state of development calls for." Maritain quotes him further as saying: "It is not a question of superimposing Christ upon the world, but of 'panchristizing' the Universe. . . . In pursuing this line of thought, one is led not merely to an enlargement of views, but to a reversal of perspective: Evil (no longer punishment for a fault, but sign and effect of Progress) and Matter (no longer a guilty and inferior element, but the 'stuff of the Spirit') take on a meaning diametrically opposed to the meaning *habitually* considered as Christian."[1] In this Maritain saw "gnosticism" and "chronolatry," a worship of the present time, of science, and of the present world at the expense of the next.

His disagreement with the ideas of Père Teilhard was shared by others, including his fellow Thomist Étienne Gilson, who described them as "a complete transposition of Christology" and "a generalization of Christ the Redeemer into a veritable Christ the evolutor." But a cry of indignation arose from Teilhard's ardent followers, and even greater consternation prevailed among the liberal proponents of Jacques Maritain's own "practical" philosophy. Many of them felt that he had not understood the development of the very trends he himself had done so much to inspire. Even so, *Aspects de la France*, a rightist organ and one of his harshest critics, conceded that Maritain's reflections constituted "the best book on the crisis in the Church since the Council began." When it appeared, there was great debate and soul-searching among Catholic intellectuals, and within a month it was listed as the best-selling work of nonfiction in France.

This did not prevent Jacques from being depressed by the reactions to his book, for it was clear that many of those who

[1] From Teilhard de Chardin, *Lettres à Léontine Zanta* (Paris: Desclée de Brouwer, 1965), pp. 127–28.

had followed him politically had not followed him philosoph-
ically. More painful to him was the confirmation of his impression that the great teachings of Aquinas which he had
tried to spread all his life had fallen into disfavor. Even in
Catholic institutions of learning few courses were being offered specifically on the works of Aquinas; in secular universities the lights were being focused on ideas concerning
the nature and origins of man expounded by the existentialist
Sartre or the anthropologist Lévi-Strauss, while in the political
and social fields stress was placed on those of Marx or
Marcuse.

Jacques Maritain did not live to learn of the renewed
interest in Aquinas that became evident at the time of the
seven hundredth anniversary of Saint Thomas' death in 1974.
He would, no doubt, have been gratified to note that the
tide was already turning in the other direction. The German
Jesuit Karl Rahner, who had blended Thomism with the
thought of such modern philosophers as Kant, Heidegger, and
Fichte, wrote that "it was not Thomas himself who was
rejected, but Thomism as the only legitimate school of theology and philosophy." In America, there were new ap-
praisals of Aquinas. In the opinion of the theologian Avery
Dulles: "He was a man of his time. He restated the whole
body of Catholic dogma in terms that made sense to a person
whose commitment was to Aristotelian philosophy. He
showed how a synthesis between dogma and philosophy can
be made creatively." Although the Protestant philosopher
Ronald Nash did not agree with Aquinas' epistemological
concept that sensory perception is the basis of all knowledge,
he nevertheless wrote: "I endorse his ideal. Christians ought
to be engaged in developing a view of life and the world as
a whole, in showing the implications of Christian theism for
every area of knowledge. No one before him and few since
have developed any world view—theistic or secular—as complete as his."

Jacques Maritain made his last trip to the United States in September 1966. This was at the time of the terminal illness and death of his and Raïssa's friend Arthur Lourié. He reached Princeton in time to make the composer's funeral arrangements himself, and to console and reassure the widow, who was living in the Maritains' former home on Linden Lane. As he told everyone that this was his "farewell visit," friends flocked from far and near to see him. Among them was Robert Hutchins, now chief executive officer of the Fund for the Republic, and his associate John Cogley, a former editor of *The Commonweal.* Joseph Evans came from Notre Dame, André Girard and Marshall Suther from New York. During this stay in Princeton, Jacques had his last meeting with John Nef, who arrived from Chicago with his wife to lunch with his old friend. Another day Jacques went with Jean Labatut to visit the Raïssa Maritain Library in the Stuart Country Day School, a handsome building of which Professor Labatut was the architect. It had been opened in October 1963 and Jacques had wanted to attend the dedication, but his doctor had advised against his making the transatlantic crossing at that time. Now at last he had come, and was much touched to find so many of Raïssa's writings assembled by the Sisters of the Sacred Heart in the beautiful library that bears her name.

After his return to France, Jacques rarely left Toulouse except for his annual visit to Kolbsheim via Paris. He continued his seminars for the Little Brothers and his writing. He had said that *The Peasant of the Garonne* was his "last testament," but was to see published two more sizable volumes: *On the Grace and Humanity of Christ* and *On the Church of Christ;* both were the development of views contained in embryo in *The Peasant of the Garonne.* Because he wished to devote his time and strength to these last books, he asked to be excused from visits and interviews, and said that his close friend Father Henry Bars would speak for him on any important matter.

In his literary work at Toulouse, Jacques had for some time the help of his godson Willard Hill, who had joined his life to that of the Little Brothers some years before. Due to his age at the time, he had not been able to become a member of their congregation, which, because of the rigors of their life, took into the novitiate only younger men. But he had devoted his time and efforts to modest publications to explain the life of the Fraternities and their spiritual ideas; many of these he translated into English. He also helped Jacques with his correspondence, and my letters from Willard often included messages from Jacques. At Toulouse there was a Dominican convent of uncloistered contemplative women of the Regular Third Order of Catherine dei Ricci, who were first established near Meudon and had known Jacques, Raïssa, and Vera. Especially in his later years, these Sisters also gave Jacques invaluable secretarial assistance.

The Little Brothers themselves helped him in every way and were always mindful of his comfort and needs. When the Dominican Fathers sold the property on which the Little Brothers had their school for theological and philosophical studies, the Brothers moved to a new site a bit farther down the road. Their cabins were rebuilt much as before and enclosed in a circle of evergreen trees. They now built—with their own hands, as always—a new chapel of reddish wood, simple but finely designed. Nearby Jacques again had his living quarters in two small rooms behind the Brothers' place of assembly. In his study were built the shelves needed for his many books and a cabinet for his papers; there was a comfortable reclining chair and a footstool before it. Again on his desk were his two favorite photographs of Raïssa; a few other pictures of friends were on the wall or along the top of the bookcases.

In these austere surroundings, Jacques continued to live

and write. He was eighty-nine years old when his book *On the Church of Christ* appeared; it was written in measured terms and moderate tone and with his customary eloquence. As his friend Father Raymond Bruckberger said: "Some doctors hold that the cells of the brain cannot be renewed. . . . As one saw Maritain's body diminish, his intellect was like a great flame on a little candle that is burning toward its end."

Jacques described the purpose of his book on the Church as the attempt of a philosopher or a "research worker" to place before the mind the "mystery of the Church in the light of the Second Vatican Council." In it, he makes some interesting distinctions between the holiness and inerrancy of the Church herself and the sinfulness and fallibility of her members, including those of her personnel. He follows Saint Paul in holding that the Church is a person, not a collective entity endowed analogically with a "moral personality," but really a person, essentially and absolutely unique, who cannot err or deceive in instructing the faithful in matters of faith and morals.

He then examines a number of thorny problems arising from the fact that some members of the Church's personnel are known to have erred in their private lives, or to have been mistaken in the exercise of their authority received from the Church, or even to have interpreted doctrine on their own responsibility and beyond the teachings of the magisterium, the Pope and bishops as a body. Most interesting are the views he offers on the respective roles of the clergy and of the laity. He believes that it is right and normal, and especially required by the present age, for the priest, while remaining a priest, to mix freely in the common life of men and to take part in the social and cultural activities of the day, provided he does not forget that his first work is to save souls.

The Second Vatican Council, he says, has particularly called the attention of Christians to their share in the priesthood of the clergy and their status as "the people of God." This is exercised in union with the Church's ministers by the offering of the Eucharist, by partaking in the other sacraments, by prayer and thanksgiving, by self-sacrifice and active charity. It is a mistake, however, for laymen to imagine that they are following the spirit of the Council by depreciating the role of the ministerial or hierarchical priesthood.

In discussing the temporal work of the laity, Maritain considers it one of the great accomplishments of the Council to have awakened Christian consciences to what is required of them. It is up to laymen to take the initiative in political movements combating social evils and injustice, and to this task they should bring enlightened theological, philosophical, and historical knowledge. He disapproves political organizations for such purposes created and directed by members of the clergy desirous of exercising a new apostolate in this way. For clerics to regiment the laity and direct their own energies to becoming leaders in the temporal sphere seems to him likely to give rise to a new form of clericalism as undesirable as the old. In Maritain's opinion, our civilization has the chance to rise beyond capitalism and communist totalitarianism to work for changes both in structural and moral order if Christian laymen, in cooperation with their friends of other spiritual families, endeavor to bring this about—but as laymen and acting on their own responsibility.

These are but a few features of Jacques Maritain's book on the Church, which goes deeply into a number of ecumenical, historical, and dogmatic subjects. In matters concerning the attributes, structure, and functions of the Church, he adheres to the views of Cardinal Journet, the Swiss theologian, who played an important role at the Vatican Council in formulating its dogmatic pronouncement on the constitution of the Church.

After he finished this book, Jacques still had another in mind, and began to prepare for publication his seminars for the Little Brothers at Toulouse (as mentioned earlier, *Ap-*

proches sans Entraves appeared posthumously). He was becoming increasingly feeble, he wrote, and had to walk with a
cane. The last letter I had from him was written in May 1969,
when he had suffered a great blow in the death of Willard
Hill. He was Jacques's last link with life at Meudon, for
Willard had remained attached to him personally and to his
interests during the intervening years and later at Toulouse.
Although Willard had suffered from lung trouble for several
years, he had continued to work calmly on translations and
on the publications of the Fraternities up to the last. He died
at a hospital at Aix-en-Provence and was buried at Marseilles
in the habit of the Little Brothers of Jesus.

Late in 1969, Jacques Maritain, the "inveterate layman,"
decided that he himself would become a member of the congregation of the Little Brothers and, exceptionally, this was
permitted. Because of his age and the condition of his health,
he was not able to go away for the year required to the novitiate of the congregation—first situated in Africa where Father de Foucauld died, but since Catholic institutions could
not remain in Algeria after its independence, now located in
a desert-like place in Spain some distance out of Saragossa.
Special arrangements were made for Jacques to make his
novitiate where he was, at the house of studies in Toulouse.
At the end of a year he took the usual vows and received
the habit. By this time he was very frail, and as it seemed
dangerous for him to be left alone at night, he was moved
to a cabin exactly opposite the chapel where several of the
Brothers had their rooms.

Remarkable as it may seem, Jacques made one more trip
to Paris and to Kolbsheim in January of 1973, some three
months before he died. In Paris he went to the office of
Desclée de Brouwer to make some arrangements about his
books. As he left, he found awaiting him a photographer who
wished to take his picture. Although it was suggested that this
be done at the Desclée office, I am told that Jacques smiled

and said that he had another background in mind; could he be taken there? He wanted to go to the Jardin des Plantes to the exact spot where he and Raïssa had met during their student days when they were trying to decide whether or not life was worth living. It was in this setting that the last photograph of Jacques was taken.

After a brief visit to his friends at Kolbsheim, to look once more at mementos of Raïssa, and to visit her grave, he returned to Toulouse. He failed rapidly after this and died suddenly of a heart attack on April 28, 1973, at the age of ninety-one, cared for to the last by the generous men with whom he had cast his lot.

In a simple wooden coffin, Jacques's body was taken to the chapel and set before the altar, where the community prayed beside it. When time came for the funeral services in Toulouse, so many people wished to attend that it was decided to hold them outdoors at an improvised altar before the Dominican provincial house nearby. There the sons and daughters of Saint Dominic appeared from many parts of France to pay special honors to a man linked to them by so many friendships and endeavors in common.

As Jacques had expressed the wish to be buried beside Raïssa, his body then was taken to Kolbsheim, accompanied by eight of the Little Brothers. There it was received with emotion by Alexandre and Antoinette Grunelius and placed in the private chapel where Jacques had knelt so often. He had asked to be buried as a poor man, for the simplest of services to be held, and for only his intimates to be present. It proved impossible to follow the last of these requests, for the chapel held not more than twenty people, and within a short time so many arrived in the small Alsatian village it became apparent that at least a hundred persons would attend. From Rome, Pope Paul—who on the day following Jacques's death had spoken in Saint Peter's Square of his grief at the loss of this "great philosopher, this man of prayer and poverty"—sent his private secretary, Monsignor Macchi, to take part in the last rites. The Swiss Cardinal Journet came and the French Cardinal Daniélou. Father Voillaume, founder of the Little Brothers of Jesus, was there, and the new prior of the congregation, Father René Page. There were also a number of bishops, the heads of religious orders of men and women, priests and nuns, professors of the Sorbonne and the University of Fribourg, friends from Paris, Strasbourg, and Kolbsheim.

Arrangements had to be made quickly for a larger place. There being no Catholic parish in Kolbsheim, the offer of the local Lutheran community for the use of the Protestant church was gratefully accepted. There on one of the first beautiful days of early May, Jacques's body was carried along the country road in an open cart drawn by the Little Brothers in their gray habits. The funeral mass was said in the Lutheran church by the superior of the Little Brothers with nine other priests concelebrating. As Jacques had requested that there be no eulogies, Professor Olivier Lacombe read from manuscript the beautiful translation that Jacques had made of Solomon's Song of Songs, and the venerable Cardinal Journet three passages from Jacques's own writings: on corporal death, on contemplation, and on Saint Thomas Aquinas.

Afterward Jacques's coffin, followed silently by the cortege on foot, was taken by the Little Brothers to the quiet cemetery of Kolbsheim, some distance from the village. Following simple prayers recited in unison by the assembly, Jacques was laid to rest beside Raïssa, and on his grave was placed a bough of hawthorn, the first blossom of the budding spring.

Afterword

Following Jacques Maritain's death, tributes were paid to him in the press and radio of many countries. He was hailed as one of the century's most influential philosophers and intellectuals, a man whose writings and teaching had made almost as much impact on the secular as on the religious world. Not only those who shared his faith, but numerous non-Catholics and non-religious persons wrote or spoke of the inspiration they had drawn from his lofty and humanist views.

Those of us who were his personal friends mourned in a special way the understanding, self-effacing man who in the midst of a hard-working and often harried life had somehow managed to keep in touch and to reach out to us at crucial moments in our lives. When his friends came together after he had gone, one always heard some new incident of his kindness and consideration, of his intellectual courtesy, of his warmhearted and often amusing ways. In our sense of loss it was a comfort to talk to others who had known him, and I began to plan this book.

In Paris, in July 1973, some three months after Jacques's death, I set out on a sort of pilgrimage to two places he called home in his last years and where I knew his memory was kept alive. So late that month I went to Toulouse to visit the study center of the Little Brothers of Jesus. Descending from the air, I saw for the first time the pleasant pattern formed by the rosy-red brick buildings of the city on the Garonne, the slow, brown, rather sullen river, and the charming Canal du Midi bordered here and there by dense, tall trees. Distinguishable from above were two buildings: the capitol or town hall, and Saint Sernin, one of the noblest Romanesque churches in meridional France. Somewhere I had read that although Thomas Aquinas had died and was buried at Fossanuova, Italy, on his way to the Council of Lyons in 1274, some hundred years later his body had been transported by his brother Dominicans to their convent in Toulouse and later removed to the Church of Saint Sernin (Saturninus). How fitting, I thought, that Jacques Maritain, his most ardent twentieth-century advocate and defender, had chosen to spend his last years and to die in this same city.

The taxi which took me from the Blagnac airport to my hotel ran first through faceless suburbs, then into a metropolis of wide avenues and verdant trees. The hotel was on a busy thoroughfare in the heart of the bustling commercial district, and through the open window of my room rose the sound of traffic, of banging shutters as shops were closed for the day, and of voices speaking in the curious but fascinating accent of Languedoc.

My first concern was to reach the Little Brothers of Jesus, to whom I had written beforehand to ask if I might be received. A quiet voice answered the telephone, saying that I was expected and to come at a time most convenient to me. As the Brothers lived at some distance from the center of the city, I made an appointment for early the following morning.

When this settled, I left the hotel to explore a bit of the nearby quarter. Not far away was the Church of Saint Sernin, and as it was still open, I went inside and saw the great clear nave of the church, the barrel roof of stone, the fine effect of the round arches and pillars in the triforium, the very deep and narrow choir. As I sat there for some time in the twilight, I felt in those long vistas before me a kind of wholesome sanctity, of manly gravity, in keeping with the spirit of the great medieval thinker who had been entombed in the crypt below.

Early the next day, I took a taxi to the Avenue Lacordaire. Passing through the city, it traveled through the outlying districts, and finally turned from the paved street of a dusty suburb into a dirt road. Although assured by the driver that he knew the right address, I found myself dumped before a large modern building which I could not reconcile in appearance with the descriptions I had heard of the quarters of the Little Brothers. After ringing a bell at the door, I was not surprised to learn that the Little Brothers did not live there; it was the provincial house of the Dominicans. Courteously directed to a site farther down the road, I entered on a path through an open field bordered with tall grass and Queen Anne's lace. At its end, within its enclosure of trees, were the cabins of the Brothers; one of them stood outside, waiting for me. After a friendly welcome, he led me into the assembly room of the largest cabin. Here he insisted on my having coffee, which he prepared as he answered my questions concerning Jacques's years at Toulouse and especially about the quarters most closely connected with him. The Brother also told me a great deal about the Little Brothers themselves, their aims, their life and rules.

After this, he showed me the little cabin where Jacques died and then, opposite it, the chapel where he worshiped daily. As we entered I saw the good proportions and taste with which this house of prayer was built with the humblest materials by those who make it the focus of their lives. The pointed ceiling is of skillfully mitered laths, supported by crossbeams of a darker color; the adobe-colored walls and plain glass windows convey a feeling of freshness and light, and most impressive is the altar in the center, a huge rectangular block of rough stone, banded near the floor with an inset of colored tiles.

We remained in the chapel for some time before going

back to the assembly room to talk a little longer. There the Brother showed me some photographs of Jacques made in Toulouse, and gave me the address of the photographer who had the negatives. With his help, I made an appointment for the following morning with Monsieur Dieuzadé, and found in him a great admirer of Jacques Maritain who had taken photographs, he told me, whenever Jacques had been persuaded to let him do so. He had a number of these, and going with him through his files, I selected a few of which I wanted copies. Returning to the Blagnac airport that afternoon, I was happy to have learned more of the friendships and affection that surrounded Jacques in his last days.

A week later, I set out to visit another place associated with Jacques over the years. I was met at Strasbourg by his goddaughter, Madame Grunelius, who drove me some fifteen miles away to the home of which Jacques, Raïssa, and Vera had been so fond. Arriving there, I saw before me the handsome seventeenth- and eighteenth-century château which, after it came into the hands of the Grunelius family, had been restored and redecorated by the Austrian architect and painter Victor Hammer. On entering, I was greeted by the Baron Grunelius with a kindness and hospitality that matched those of his wife. Staying with them at the time was one of the Brothers from Toulouse who had been most closely associated with Jacques in his last days. He joined us in the great library with its book-lined walls and, at the enormous desk piled high with Jacques's papers on which the Brother and Madame Grunelius had been working, we talked for hours of our departed friend.

The library opened out on gardens with tall hedges and beds of flowers in bloom and, beyond its parapets, to an expanse of fertile fields and the forests and mountains of the Vosges. After tea, Madame Grunelius and I continued our reminiscences of the Maritains as we walked around the long, graveled paths. She showed me the guest house where the

Maritains stayed, with its living quarters and the big room with the huge table where Jacques had worked. Many of his books and papers are kept there, and it is now the Maritain Center at Kolbsheim. Very close to the guest house is the beautiful chapel designed by Victor Hammer and built after the Gruneliuses took possession of the estate. From it, Raïssa had been buried, and as we know, Jacques had also wished his funeral services to be held there.

As Madame Grunelius and I returned in her car to Strasbourg we passed, at some distance down the road, the village cemetery where Jacques and Raïssa are buried. It was too late to visit it that day, but the next morning I returned alone. Under the tall cypress trees, I found the two little graves. My heart was heavy as I thought of these two lives—their great mutual love and the love they had shown to so many others, their long years of striving to make the world better. Had it all ended here? Then I remembered something that Jacques had written long ago in his *Letter on Independence:*

"The master foresters work far ahead and with an exact plan for the future state of the forest even though it will not be seen by their own or their children's eyes. . . ."